Strangely Bright

STRANGELY BRIGHT

Can You Love God and *Enjoy This World?*

JOE RIGNEY

WHEATON, ILLINOIS

Scripture quotations are from the ESV® Bible (The Holy Bible, English Standard Version®), copyright © 2001 by Crossway, a publishing ministry of Good News Publishers. Used by permission. All rights reserved.

All emphases in Scripture quotations have been added by the author.

Trade paperback ISBN: 978-1-4335-6935-7
ePub ISBN: 978-1-4335-6938-8
PDF ISBN: 978-1-4335-6936-4
Mobipocket ISBN: 978-1-4335-6937-1

Library of Congress Cataloging-in-Publication Data

Names: Rigney, Joe, 1982- author.
Title: Strangely bright : can you love God and enjoy this world? / Joe Rigney.
Description: Wheaton, Illinois : Crossway, 2020. | Includes bibliographical references and index.
Identifiers: LCCN 2019043104 (print) | LCCN 2019043105 (ebook) | ISBN 9781433569357 (trade paperback) | ISBN 9781433569364 (pdf) | ISBN 9781433569371 (mobi) | ISBN 9781433569388 (epub)
Subjects: LCSH: God (Christianity)—Worship and love. | Hedonism–Religious aspects–Christianity. | God (Christianity)–Knowableness.
Classification: LCC BV4817 .R54 2020 (print) | LCC BV4817 (ebook) | DDC 231–dc23
LC record available at https://lccn.loc.gov/2019043104
LC ebook record available at https://lccn.loc.gov/2019043105

Crossway is a publishing ministry of Good News Publishers.

To Jack Joseph Rigney
A very good and perfect gift

Contents

Introduction

This little book has a simple purpose. I want to address a problem that I suspect many readers have felt, even if you've never named it. If you're a faithful Christian, this problem or tension has probably haunted you, playing at the back of your mind and affecting you in subtle ways.

Let me introduce the problem by telling you a little of my story. When I was in ninth grade my family joined a church plant in our mid-sized West Texas town. My formative high school years were spent in that church. One of the things I remember our pastor saying over and over again is that life is not about me. It's about God. It's about Jesus. I remember him telling us that in the book of Ezekiel, God repeatedly says that he does all the things he does—creating the world, saving his people, punishing sin, judging his enemies—for one main reason: so that people will know that God is the Lord. God, it seems, is radically God-centered. He does everything that he does for the sake of his name, for his glory. This biblical truth made an impact on me, not only because of what was said, but because of *how* it was said. From my pastor to the youth leaders to the youth-camp speakers that were frequently brought in, there was an intensity, a zeal, a fire in the eyes that communicated to my high-school self that the things that we were talking about were the most important things in life. Jesus is real. Jesus saves. Jesus restores. Jesus gives us significance. And he does all of it for the sake of his name.

When I went off to college, the biblical truth that everything is about God was filled up and filled out. I was already primed for it. I became familiar with the ministry of John Piper, a pastor in Minneapolis. Piper put his finger on a tension that I'd felt in my own life, a tension between the biblical truth that everything is about God and the experiential truth that I wanted to be happy. I knew that I wanted to be happy and that I wanted my life to matter, to count for something. The desire for happiness and significance was like breathing. And Piper showed me, as he's shown thousands of others through his preaching and writing, that in the end, there is no tension between God's passion for his glory and my passion for my happiness. This is because God made me so that I would find my deepest happiness in him. In fact, Piper summarized his biblical conclusions in a simple yet life-changing statement: God is most glorified in us when we are most satisfied in him. That truth went off like an explosion in my soul. All my passion for meaning, significance, happiness, and joy was channeled into a passion to glorify God by enjoying him above all earthly things.

After college, I made my way north to Minneapolis to be trained and equipped as a pastor at The Bethlehem Institute (now Bethlehem College & Seminary), an apprenticeship program at Piper's church. I came to saturate myself in Christian Hedonism, the provocative term that Piper used to describe the biblical truth that we glorify God by seeking our highest pleasure in him. I wanted to see what this approach to life and ministry looked like on the ground. I loved the mission statement of the church and the school: "We exist to spread a passion for the supremacy of God in all things for the joy of all peoples through Jesus Christ." And in God's providence, not only did I attend seminary at Bethlehem, but I now teach at Bethlehem College & Seminary and pastor a church in the Twin Cities. And I'm still a Christian Hedonist, and I still love that mission. And though you may not use the same words, I assume that if you're a Christian, you resonate at some level with those truths. The supremacy of God in all things. For the joy of all peoples. Jesus Christ at the center.

The Experiential Tension

This brings me back to this book. As I said, Christian Hedonism resolved one tension, the tension between God's passion for his glory and my passion for happiness. But it also created another tension. Maybe you'll hear it in a passage like Psalm 73:25–26:

> Whom have I in heaven but you?
>   And there is nothing on earth that I desire besides you.
> My flesh and my heart may fail,
>   but God is the strength of my heart and my portion
>   forever.

You can hear the Christian Hedonism in the passage. God is the strength of my heart. I desire nothing besides him. He's my all and my everything. He's my portion forever. Christians love to sing songs like that. And yet if we stop and think about it, do we really mean it? "On earth there is nothing I desire besides you." Really? Not your family? Not your friends? Not your hobbies? Not your favorite food? If we're honest, don't we speak out of both sides of our mouth? On the one hand, we say, "I desire nothing but you, God," and on the other hand, we say, "Except for all the other things I desire." And there's the tension that produced this book: how does a single-minded pursuit of the glory of God fit with a real and deep enjoyment of created things? Let me get more concrete: how does the rock-bottom biblical truth that you are called to glorify God by delighting in him above everything else relate to your enjoyment of good friends, pork tamales, the laughter of children, West Texas sunsets, marital love, and college football?

My guess is that many of you have asked that question and felt this tension too. You're torn by your desire to love and honor God above all things and your unavoidable and inescapable delight in earthly things. You've felt a kind of low-grade guilt whenever you *really* enjoy an earthly pleasure. Maybe you live with a perpetual sense that you're not enjoying God "enough" (whatever that means) or that you're enjoying his gifts "too much" (whatever that means). Maybe you've begun to treat created things like hot potatoes, looking at your delight in physical affection and chocolate ice cream and a walk around the lake in early fall with a wary and skeptical eye, because you wonder whether it's too precious to you. Maybe you have a sense that as you grow in holiness, as you become more like Jesus, that your enjoyment of fresh raspberries and lively conversation with friends and gardening in the springtime ought to diminish, ought to grow dim, because you're increasingly satisfied with God *alone*.

Often these vague feelings are rooted in our beliefs and convictions. We know that God is infinitely valuable, and that our family and friends and food are not, and therefore, we feel that there ought to be a larger gap between our love for *them* and our love for *him*. Knowing this, we sometimes try to suppress our joy in the things of earth so that they don't compete and get in the way of our love for Christ. Or, on the other side of things, we try to suppress our *grief* whenever we lose gifts that are very

14

dear to us—like a spouse, or a parent, or child—because we don't want to dishonor God by treating them as idols. We fear that our sadness and pain reveal that these earthly gifts are too precious to us. This is the experiential tension, and if you've felt it, this book is for you.

The Biblical Tension

It's important to note that this isn't just a tension in our experience. It's a tension in the Bible. In fact, for most of us, we feel the experiential tension precisely because we want to believe and obey God's word. So think with me about the following passages of Scripture.

> Whatever gain I had, I counted as loss for the sake of Christ. Indeed, *I count everything as loss because of the surpassing worth of knowing Christ Jesus my Lord.* For his sake I have suffered the loss of all things and *count them as rubbish*, in order that I may gain Christ. (Phil. 3:7–8)

> If then you have been raised with Christ, seek the things that are above, where Christ is, seated at the right hand of God. *Set your minds on things that are above, not on things that are on earth.* (Col. 3:1–2)

> Whom have I in heaven but you?
> And there is nothing on earth that I desire besides you.
> My flesh and my heart may fail,
> but God is the strength of my heart and my portion forever. (Ps. 73:25–26)

Let's call these the *Totalizing* passages, since they express a total and complete devotion to God in Christ. Everything is rubbish compared to Christ. Don't set your mind on things below. Desire nothing besides God. That's one message in the Bible. Now consider passages like this:

> As for the rich in this present age, charge them not to be haughty, nor to set their hopes on the uncertainty of riches, but on God, *who richly provides us with everything to enjoy.* (1 Tim. 6:17)

> *For everything created by God is good*, and nothing is to be rejected if it is received with thanksgiving. (1 Tim. 4:4)

> *Every good gift and every perfect gift is from above*, coming down from the Father of lights, with whom there is no variation or shadow due to change. (James 1:17)

Let's call these the *Things of Earth* passages, since they express the goodness of enjoying created things. And when we place these passages side by side, we're faced with a conundrum—which is it: *Only* desire God? Or enjoy *everything* God richly provides? Count everything as rubbish? Or receive everything with thanksgiving? Set your mind on things above? Or enjoy the good and perfect gifts that have come down from above? This is not just a tension in your life; it's a tension in the Bible.

Overview

The seven chapters in this book seek to resolve both the biblical and the experiential tension. Each chapter is anchored in a passage of Scripture. We begin with Psalm 19 and explore the ways that God's word and God's world work together in order to show us what he's like and teach us how to relate to him.

In chapter 2 we walk through the early chapters of Genesis and reflect on God's original design and purpose for the world. There we see that God is truly a hedonist at heart, scattering pleasures of every kind throughout his creation both for our enjoyment and for the fulfillment of his mission.

In the third chapter we consider two complementary approaches to God and his gifts: an integrated approach based in Proverbs 24:13–14 and a comparative approach based in Romans 1 and Psalm 73:25–26. Our calling is to enjoy God in everything and everything in God, while knowing deep in our bones that Jesus is better than every earthly good.

In chapter 4 we unpack the importance of setting our minds on things above, from Colossians 3:1–4. This heavenly mind-set is both oriented by Christ and profoundly earthy, and works itself out in rhythms of direct and indirect godwardness.

In chapter 5 we consider two crucial tests of our enjoyment of the things of earth. Both self-denial (Luke 9:23–25) and generosity (1 Tim. 6:17–19) serve our joy in God and his gifts by guarding us against the dangers of ingratitude, idolatry, and sinful indulgence.

In chapter 6 we take a long, hard look at suffering, death, and the loss of good gifts. Paul's words in 2 Corinthians 1:3–11 expose some of the challenges of suffering and loss as well as the only source of true and lasting comfort.

Finally, in chapter 7, we get concrete and particular as we explore one of my favorite things of earth—the game of baseball. For me, baseball is a thick and layered joy, a complex pleasure that illustrates many of the truths in this book. My hope is that this final chapter provides a helpful model as you seek to enjoy your own things of earth for the glory of God.

In all of this, my desire is simple. I want to work with you for your joy. Your joy in your family. Your joy in your friends. Your joy in your pancakes and eggs, your steak and potatoes, your chips and your salsa. Your joy in your camping trips, workouts, and Spotify playlist. Your joy in the Bible, in worship services, and in the quiet moments before you fall asleep. Your joy in your job, your hobbies, and your daily routine.

And in and through all these things, I want to work with you for your joy in the living and personal God who delivered you from sin and death through the work of his Son and Holy Spirit and gives you all these things that you might enjoy him *and* them and him *in* them forever.

1

What the Heavens Declare

Psalm 19 begins with one of the most famous verses in the Bible: "The heavens declare the glory of God." The first half of the psalm celebrates God's glory in nature—in the heavens (v. 1), in the sun's course across the sky (vv. 4, 6), in the similarities between the sun and a warrior and a bridegroom (v. 5). This revelation has gone out to the entire world so that there is no place where God's revelation is not heard (vv. 2–4). In other words, the psalm begins with a celebration of what theologians call "general revelation." General revelation includes all the ways that God reveals himself in creation—in the ordinary course of nature and the general course of history. In other words, it's not just the heavens that declare the glory of God. *Everything* that God has made declares the glory of God. The apostle Paul tells us that God's "invisible attributes, namely, his eternal power and divine nature, have been clearly perceived, ever since the creation of the world, *in the things that have been made*" (Rom. 1:20). In other words, made things make invisible attributes visible. Created things make eternal things perceivable. God's own power and righteousness and beauty and wisdom and mercy are invisible attributes. We can't see them directly. But when we see a tornado tear across the plains, we see his power. When we stand on a giant mountain, we feel the firmness and stability of his righteousness. When we watch the sun set over the Pacific Ocean, we see his beauty. When we witness the magnificent intricacy of the food chain—deer eating grass and then being eaten by lions—we see his inscrutable wisdom and mercy over all that he has made. Made things make invisible attributes visible.

That's what we mean by general revelation, and by its nature, it is pervasive and constant. It's accessible to all men everywhere. "There is no speech, nor are there words, whose voice is not heard" (Ps. 19:3). As C. S. Lewis said, "We may ignore, but we can nowhere evade the presence of God. The world is crowded with Him. He walks everywhere incognito."[1] Jonathan Edwards, an eighteenth-century American pastor and theologian, testified that he believed that the whole universe, heaven and earth, from top to bottom and front to back is filled with "images of divine things, as full as a language is of words."[2] By this, he meant that everything in creation is communication from God about God. God speaks to us everywhere and in everything.

Earthly Categories for Spiritual Things

General revelation works both directly and indirectly. It works directly by creating categories in our minds and hearts for knowing God. This is direct because we move straight from the made thing to God himself. How do the heavens declare the glory of God? Through their size and majesty. The vastness of the heavens points to the greatness of God. Or the beauty of a sunset gives us a visual picture of the beauty and holiness of God. Or the sun's perpetual and constant shining images God's constant and everlasting goodness. In each case, we move straight from the made thing to God himself. Our experience of the world gives us categories for knowing God and his word.

And not just God himself. General revelation gives us categories for knowing many aspects of the spiritual life. Consider Psalm 1.

> Blessed is the man
>> who walks not in the counsel of the wicked,
> nor stands in the way of sinners,
>> nor sits in the seat of scoffers;
> but his delight is in the law of the LORD,
>> and on his law he meditates day and night.
>
> He is like a tree
>> planted by streams of water
> that yields its fruit in its season,
>> and its leaf does not wither.
> In all that he does, he prospers.
> The wicked are not so,
>> but are like chaff that the wind drives away. (Ps. 1:1–4)

In this psalm, fruitful trees are audiovisual aids to help us understand the blessed and righteous man, just as tumbleweeds are audiovisual aids to help us understand the wicked. Men are like trees, and different trees help us understand different types of men. This is why God made the world he did and gave us eyes and ears and a nose and a mouth and skin. Our senses are designed to take in the world, and then our minds and hearts are designed to connect our experience of the natural world to the spiritual world and the God who governs both.

In the course of writing this book, I found the perfect opportunity to illustrate the way that our experiential knowledge of the world through general revelation helps us to understand the Bible and thus to know God more deeply. Every year, Bethlehem College & Seminary hosts a pastors' conference in Minneapolis. *In January.* And every year a few thousand pastors and church leaders journey to the land of ice and snow in order to be encouraged through worship, teaching, and fellowship. For our brethren from the South, we know that the trip is almost a rite of passage. They get to return home and regale their congregations with stories of their exploits in the frozen tundra. "The snowdrifts were up to my waist. My eyes almost froze shut. I nearly died attempting to cross the street to scavenge for food."

In January of 2019, however, the cold went to another level. The wind chill dropped down to −45 degrees. Even for native Minnesotans, that's cold. That year I told the pastors assembled there:

> You're going to go home and try to explain to your people how cold it was here. You might try to use math. You'll tell them, "You know the difference between 80 degrees and 40 degrees? It was like that temperature difference over again, and then over again—80 to 40 to 0 to -40." And they might get some idea of the cold. But you know that they won't *really* get it. You, on the other hand—you walked outside with your little Target beanie and windbreaker. Your nose hairs turned to ice in under five seconds. You lost feeling in your fingers before you made it from your car to the conference center *in the parking garage.* And because you experienced all of that, Psalm 147 now means more to you:
>
>> He sends out his command to the earth;
>>> his word runs swiftly.
>> He gives snow like wool;
>>> he scatters frost like ashes.

He hurls down his crystals of ice like crumbs;
    who can stand before his cold? (Ps. 147:15–17)

No one. No one can stand before his cold. Not you. Not me.
Our experience of nature, of general revelation, has built
categories in our minds so that we read Psalm 147 with fresh
(and frozen) eyes.[3]

A Web of Images

General revelation also works in a more *indirect* fashion. Again,
Psalm 19 shows us how. When the psalmist unpacks *how* the
heavens declare the glory of God, he turns to the sun as it jour-
neys from horizon to horizon:

In them he has set a tent for the sun,
    which comes out like a bridegroom leaving his
        chamber,
and, like a strong man, runs its course with joy.
    (Ps. 19:4–5)

Notice that the psalmist makes two comparisons. The sun is
like a bridegroom leaving his chamber and like a strong man
who runs his course with joy. David looks at the sun as it moves
across the sky, and then he looks at a groom on his wedding day,
and he sees a connection. In the brilliance of the sun, he sees the
gladness of a groom. He looks at the sun again and is reminded
of Josheb-as-hebeth, one of his mighty men, running into battle
with spear raised and eyes blazing (2 Sam. 23:8). The sun is like
the groom, and the sun is like the warrior. It's this indirect web
of images that shows us *how* the heavens declare the glory of
God. The sun is bright and triumphant, the bridegroom's face is
shining as he stands at the aisle, the warrior is intense but joyful
since he is doing what he was built to do.

This means that reality is a web of images, pictures, patterns, analogies, and metaphors all woven together by the wisdom and skill of our Creator. Metaphors and analogies operate on a principle of comparison. We set one thing next to another thing in order to better understand them both. The sun helps us to understand weddings, and weddings in turn help us to see the sun with new eyes. Warriors help us to understand bridegrooms, and bridegrooms in turn illuminate warriors. In the psalm David recognizes the likenesses among these various things of earth. They're not identical, but they are similar. And this web is held together by Christ—in him all things hold together (Col. 1:17).

Therefore, if we want to know God through general revelation, we don't always go directly to him. Instead we move horizontally between the images, among the things of earth, understanding how they relate to each other, so that the *whole* picture and experience of the world can then lead us to God. God draws us into this web of creation so that we might know him through it. It's how he reveals himself to us in a way that fits our frame.

And notice how in each of these passages, it's something *outside* the Bible that helps us to understand *the meaning* of the Bible. If you've never seen the sun move triumphantly across the sky, then Psalm 19 doesn't *mean* anything to you. If you've never seen a fruitful tree on the edge of a river or a tumbleweed blowing across the highway into a ditch, then Psalm 1 doesn't *mean* anything to you. And the reason we hold the Bethlehem Conference for Pastors and Church Leaders in January in Minnesota is that we want those pastors to *really* know the meaning of Psalm 147. No one—and I mean *no one*—can stand before his cold.

Keeping Our Metaphors Honest

At this point, it's worth briefly addressing obvious questions. If God communicates to us through creation by means of analogies, images, and metaphors, does that mean that any metaphor we come up with is a revelation from God? What keeps this way of thinking from going off the rails and becoming simply a way for people with fruitful imaginations to say all kinds of foolishness about God? These questions show why we need special revelation. Special revelation refers to the unique ways that God has revealed himself at particular times and places. It includes prophecy, visions, miracles, and God's mighty acts of redemption. The most important form of special revelation is the Bible, God's unique, inerrant, and authoritative word to human beings. Thus it's no surprise that Psalm 19 moves seamlessly from celebrating God's revelation in creation (19:1–6) to celebrating God's revelation in the Bible:

> The law of the LORD is perfect,
> reviving the soul;
> the testimony of the LORD is sure,
> making wise the simple;
> the precepts of the LORD are right,
> rejoicing the heart;
> the commandment of the LORD is pure,
> enlightening the eyes;
> the fear of the LORD is clean,
> enduring forever;
> the rules of the LORD are true,
> and righteous altogether.
> More to be desired are they than gold,
> even much fine gold;
> sweeter also than honey
> and drippings of the honeycomb.

> Moreover, by them is your servant warned;
>> in keeping them there is great reward. (19:7–11)

The written, authoritative word of God is what keeps us on the right path. It keeps our metaphors and analogies in check. The law of the Lord revives the soul, makes us wise so we don't say foolish things about God, enlightens our eyes so we see God everywhere, and guards us from error. If creation is a language in which God speaks to us through sights and sounds and smells and tastes and sensations, then Scripture is the grammar textbook for that language, the language of God. Now it doesn't give us the whole language; we're not restricted to the images of the Bible. But the Bible does show us the basics; it gives us examples so we can learn how the images of divine things work and then unleashes us, by the grace of God, to find him everywhere that he is speaking. As the old hymn says:

> This is my Father's world
> He shines in all that's fair
> In the rustling grass I hear him pass
> He speaks to me everywhere.

That's why biblical authors are always pointing us out to the world to learn what God is like and how to live. Are you anxious about food? Consider the birds, Jesus says. Are you worried about shelter and clothing? Consider the lilies of the field. Are you lazy? Solomon tells us to consider the ant. And then Jesus and Solomon explain the lesson that we are to learn from creation, and in doing so, they train us in careful interpretation of general revelation. They teach us how to read the world. They help us to see how general and special revelation work together to give us knowledge of God.

The Gospel of John

Now, the best way that I know to bring these truths together is with an extended look at a particular passage of Scripture. In John 6 Jesus utters the first of seven "I am" statements in John's Gospel: "I am the bread of life" (v. 35). Like many aspects of John's Gospel, this is a simple statement full of rich meaning. More importantly for us, this is an example of special revelation (Jesus's words in the Bible) showing us how to interpret general revelation (bread).

Let's begin by setting some background. Jesus is in the midst of his ministry. He's been gathering disciples, teaching crowds, and performing signs. Now the apostle John gives special attention to Jesus's signs. In his book, signs have particular characteristics. Signs are public, supernatural acts that reveal Jesus to his disciples and to the crowds. They are designed either to bring about faith in Jesus as the Son of God or to harden the unbelieving. These signs are explicitly identified as such in John's Gospel, confirm Christ's identity as the one sent by God, and emphasize that Jesus brings life to the world using physical representation and symbols.

John seems to focus on seven particular signs. The first is when Jesus turns water into wine at a wedding ("This, the first of his signs, Jesus did at Cana in Galilee," 2:11). The second is healing an official's son ("This was now the second sign that Jesus did," 4:54). The third is when Jesus heals the paralytic in chapter 5. We know this is a sign because in 6:2 we're told that a large crowd was following him because they had seen the signs he was doing on the sick. The fourth is when Jesus feeds five thousand people with five loaves of bread and two fish (John 6). Jesus multiplies the loaves and fish, and "when the people saw the sign that he had done, they said, 'This is indeed the Prophet who is to come into the world'" (6:14). And because they are so amazed, they want to force him to become king. As a result, Jesus withdraws into a solitary place. Later that evening, his disciples go across the sea in a boat, and Jesus walks to them on the water, and they all make it to the other side of the sea. The next day (6:22), the people realize that Jesus is gone, so they sail across the sea, "seeking Jesus" (6:24). And that brings us to the crucial passage. So let's walk through it, making observations as we go, and then draw a few conclusions at the end.

The Bread of Life

When the crowds finally find Jesus, they ask him, "When did you come here?"

> Jesus answered them, "Truly, truly, I say to you, you are seeking me, not because you saw signs, but because you ate your fill of the loaves." (6:26)

In other words, Jesus knows what these people are after. They're not seeking him because they saw public, supernatural acts that showed his glory and called forth faith. They're seeking him because they want more bread. They saw the sign, but they didn't *really* see the sign. They didn't see what the sign pointed to. All they know is that this Jesus guy can multiply bread. If they stay with him, they'll never go hungry again. They'll always have full bellies. Jesus continues:

> Do not work for the food that perishes, but for the food that endures to eternal life, which the Son of Man will give to you. For on him God the Father has set his seal. (6:27)

Jesus says, "You worked hard to find me. You went through a lot of effort in order to get another free lunch. But don't just work for food that perishes, that rots and gets moldy. Work for food that lasts, that remains, that abides to eternal life, which the Son of Man [i.e., Jesus] will give you."

> Then they said to him, "What must we do, to be doing the works of God?" Jesus answered them, "This is the work of God, that you believe in him whom he has sent." So they said to him, "Then what sign do you do, that we may see and believe you? What work do you perform?" (6:28–30)

In other words, "Show us something. Do one of those public supernatural acts and then we'll believe in you." And in case Jesus can't think of a sign to do, they have an idea:

> Our fathers ate the manna in the wilderness; as it is written, "He gave them bread from heaven to eat." (6:31)

This is a reference to a story from the Old Testament (Ex. 16). God rescued his people, the Hebrews, from slavery in Egypt. After he did so, they were out in the desert and started to grumble and complain. "We're starving. If only we'd stayed in Egypt. We had food there, but out here, we're going to die." And God graciously provided them with food. Every day they woke up to this bread-like substance on the ground. They gathered it up and had enough for one day. But if they tried to store it overnight, it bred worms and stank. It was food that perished and rotted. They had to trust God to supply it every day. They called it "manna," which is just a Hebrew word that means "What is it?" It's like you come out of your tent, and there's food on the ground, but you're not sure what it is, but you eat it, and it fills your belly, and then you name it "Whatchamacallit." The point is that God provided magic bread from heaven to his people in the wilderness.

Now Jesus shows up and multiplies bread like magic, and the people think, "Yes! Lunchtime! A new Moses! He gave our fathers bread from heaven to eat; now you give us bread from heaven to eat."

> Jesus then said to them, "Truly, truly, I say to you, it was not Moses who gave you the bread from heaven, but my Father gives you the true bread from heaven. For the bread of God is he who comes down from heaven and gives life to the world." They said to him, "Sir, give us this bread always." (John 6:32–34)

The people are fixated on filling their bellies, their natural appetite, and Jesus is trying to show them a different kind of bread. He's trying to take them deeper. They're saying, "Give us bread like Moses did." And Jesus says, "Actually Moses didn't give it to you; God did. And he wants to give you true bread from heaven, which is the person who comes down from heaven and gives life to the world." But they're not really getting it, so they say, "Yeah, yeah, whatever. Just give us this magic bread always." And then he gets explicit about what he means:

> Jesus said to them, "I am the bread of life; whoever comes to me shall not hunger, and whoever believes in me shall never thirst. But I said to you that you have seen me and yet do not believe. All that the Father gives me will come to me, and whoever comes to me I will never cast out. For I have come down from heaven, not to do my own will but the will of him who sent me. And this is the will of him who sent me, that I should lose nothing of all that he has given me, but raise it up on the last day. For this is the will of my Father, that everyone who looks on the Son and believes in

him should have eternal life, and I will raise him up on the last day." (6:35–40)

And then they start grumbling because he's not multiplying magic bread but saying that he himself is the bread. And they say, "Isn't this Jesus, the son of Joseph? We know his mom and dad. How can he say, 'I've come down from heaven'?" (see 6:41–42). Then:

> Jesus answered them, "Do not grumble among yourselves. No one can come to me unless the Father who sent me draws him. And I will raise him up on the last day. It is written in the Prophets, 'And they will all be taught by God.' Everyone who has heard and learned from the Father comes to me—not that anyone has seen the Father except he who is from God; he has seen the Father. Truly, truly, I say to you, whoever believes has eternal life. I am the bread of life. Your fathers ate the manna in the wilderness, and they died. This is the bread that comes down from heaven, so that one may eat of it and not die. I am the living bread that came down from heaven. If anyone eats of this bread, he will live forever. And the bread that I will give for the life of the world is my flesh." (6:43–51)

In other words, "Don't stumble over the sign. I'm the real bread. I don't just want to fill your belly for a few hours. I want to give you eternal life. I want you to come to me and eat the bread of life. I want you to eat living bread, to feast on me, and be truly satisfied forever."

After this, they start arguing among themselves—"What's this guy talking about?" (see 6:52). Jesus tries to explain some more, but then a number of these followers say, "We don't get it. This is too hard and complicated. We're out" (see 6:60, 66). And they turn back and no longer follow him.

What Does Bread Declare?

We can see four key truths in this story that are relevant for this book. First, as we've seen, creation is designed by God to show us what he is like. Or, to be more specific, creation is designed to reveal who Jesus is. God has designed the entire universe to reveal Jesus. Long before you and I existed, long before Jesus came in the flesh, before the Bible was written down, from the very beginning God invented something called "hunger" and something called "bread" so that some day, when Jesus showed up, we would have categories for understanding who he is. In other words, when Jesus says, "I am the bread of life," he's not finding or discovering a convenient metaphor. He's revealing the main reason that bread exists. Every growling stomach, every empty belly, every hearty meal, every satisfied hunger in the history of the world has been leading to the moment when Jesus shows up and people ask, "Who are you?" and he replies, "I am the bread of life."

Second, in this case, it's not merely that God's creation reveals who Jesus is. Human culture reveals who Jesus is. Jesus says that he is the *bread* of life, not the *grain* of life. Grain is something that God makes. Bread is something that people make out of the grain that God makes. That's what culture is—a mixture of God's creation and man's creativity. And this tells us that not only is creation designed to reveal God, but human culture is also capable of showing us what God is like. When we faithfully mingle our creative labor with God's creation, we glorify the things of earth. Bread is grain, but glorified through man's efforts. Wine is grapes, but glorified through man's efforts. While human culture is fallen and broken by sin, it is still able to be a reflection of divine wisdom and glory so that we can know who Jesus is and how we should relate to him.

Third, not only does God design reality and weave his creation and human culture together so that they reveal Jesus, but he orchestrates the history of redemption in order to reveal Jesus. By saying, "I am the bread of life," Jesus doesn't simply tap into the universal experience of hunger; he connects himself to the particular history of Israel. God's mighty acts in history and the record of those acts in the Bible all point to Christ. Why did God give his people Whatchamacallit in the wilderness? To feed them, yes. To keep them alive in a desert, yes. But, ultimately, he gave them bread from heaven so that one day Jesus could say, "I am the true bread that comes down from heaven. That story points to me. It creates a category in your mind so that you know how you should relate to me."

Finally, Jesus's words in John 6 echo in our minds and hearts every time we partake of the Lord's Supper. Theologians have often described the Lord's Supper as an edible word. Jesus is the bread of life. The bread at the Lord's Table is his body, just as the wine is his blood. At the table, God offers us special grace in the bread and wine that we receive by faith. But the special grace of the Lord's Supper flows outward to the rest of our lives. It reminds us that God's invisible attributes are revealed everywhere—in creation, in human culture, in God's mighty works of redemption. All of reality is a display of God and an invitation to know God. In showing us what God is like, the world beckons us further up and further in so that we can know *him* and love *him* and enjoy *him* through the things he has made.

2

Pleasures in the Garden

The last chapter focused on the ways that God's world and God's word work together to reveal what he is like and how we should live. In this chapter we're going to take another step in resolving the biblical and experiential tension by exploring why God filled the world with all kinds of pleasures and delights. To do this, we need to go back to the beginning. The early chapters of Genesis show us God's original design and purpose for the world. So we'll walk through this passage and see how and why God made the world in the way that he did. And because we're focused on the tension between love for God and delight in the things of earth, we want to keep the Greatest Commandment in mind as we explore Genesis 1 and 2.

Jesus gives us the Greatest Commandment in Mark 12:30: "You shall love the Lord your God with all your heart and with all your soul and with all your mind and with all your strength." Quoting the book of Deuteronomy, he tells us that we are to love God fully, unreservedly, with nothing held back. To the Greatest Commandment, we could also add the first of the Ten

Commandments: "You shall have no other gods before me" (Ex. 20:2), and we see that we must love God *fully* and *supremely*. He must be supreme in our affections, highest in our loves. And, finally, we might consider Paul's prayer in Philippians 1:9 that our love "may *abound* more and more, with knowledge and all discernment." Supreme love, full love, expanding love. This is God's call upon all of us. With that in mind, we're now ready to consider the early chapters of Genesis.

The basic story is simple. Genesis 1 provides the overview. In the beginning God creates the heavens and the earth. He spends three days forming the earth into a well-ordered cosmos and then three days filling it with all manner of inhabitants. He turns on the lights, he establishes a rhythm of day and night, he divides the world into various arenas—sky, seas, and land—and then he covers the land with fragrant and luxurious trees and grasses and flowers and foliage. Once the world is formed, he turns over the regulation of time to the great light, the lesser light, and the host of the heavens that shine in the sky. He fills the seas with tuna and trout and dolphins and giant squid, and he fills the sky with sparrows and eagles and ravens and doves. He fills the land with oxen and sheep and deer, with squirrels and rabbits and frogs, with lions and tigers and bears (Oh, my). And he caps it all off by creating man in his own image, dividing the human race into two sexes—male and female—and giving them dominion over all that is under the sun. On the seventh day, God rests from his creative labor and sanctifies the Sabbath as a day of rest and gladness.

Genesis 2 then revisits the creation of man and woman, showing the full picture more clearly, as God forms man from the dust, places him in paradise in the land of Eden, establishes a covenant of life with him, gives him the task of naming the world, and then builds a woman out of a rib from his side. Genesis 2 ends with a wedding, as God unites the man and woman together as one flesh before him, called to be fruitful and multiply and fill his very good world.

God's Freedom and Creativity

This story is worth much reflection. First, consider God's freedom. Nothing beyond his own wisdom and good pleasure constrained his creativity. "Our God is in the heavens; he does all that he pleases" (Ps. 115:3). In choosing to create, in creating in this particular way, in forming and filling the world as he did, God accomplished exactly what he wanted to do, which means that we may look at what he did to see what he desired. Given God's absolute freedom and sovereignty, his actions always reveal his pleasure.

So when we consider the heavens and the earth, we are seeing the fruit of God's wisdom and creativity. When the divine artist painted his masterpiece, these are the lines that he drew. When the heavenly composer conducted his symphony, these are the notes he chose. Drawing from the inexhaustible depths of his life and wisdom and joy, this world—this magnificent collection of cows and canaries, of maple syrup and lemon meringue, of snow-capped peaks and fertile valleys, of bubbles and babies and billowing clouds, of hydrangeas and rhubarb and chipmunks and cedar, of lightning and thunder and rainbows and dew—this world is the one that the Maker of heaven and earth called forth from nothing and formed into glory.

The Goodness of Our Limitations

Second, the glory of this world includes our limitations as creatures. When God created human beings as bearers of his image, he created us as bodily and temporal beings. We exist in space, and we exist in time. We live *here*, and we live *now*. We are bound to one location, and we experience reality in a succession of moments. We are both embodied and en-storied creatures. In fact, when God formed man from the dust of the ground, he made his body first, and *then* breathed into him the breath of life so that man became a living creature (Gen. 2:5–8). We are not spirits imprisoned in bodies. In fact, the separation of the spirit from the body is so alien to our nature that God calls it "death." To be truly and fully human is to be an embodied soul and an ensouled body.

This means that temporality, limitation, and finitude are not defects to be overcome. Our existence in time and space and bodies is not a bug; it's a feature designed by infinite wisdom for God's glory and our joy. God is never frustrated by our finitude. He's not hamstrung by our limitations. Our creatureliness poses no barrier to him. "He knows our frame; he remembers that we are dust" (Ps. 103:14), and *he does not despise us for it*. He made us this way, and he thinks it was a grand idea.

A World of Pleasures

Third, as we consider Genesis 1 and 2, we can't help but notice that the beauty and goodness of creation is God's gift to us. He fills his world with pleasures and delights for his people. As we survey the chapters, we can classify these pleasures into three categories.

SENSIBLE PLEASURES—THINGS WE ENJOY

First, in Genesis 2:9, the trees in the garden are described as "pleasant to the sight and good for food." They're attractive to the eye and delicious to taste *by God's design*. And then a few

verses later, God issues his first commands to man, and they
have to do with these fruitful trees:

> And the LORD God commanded the man, saying, "You may
> surely eat of every tree of the garden, but of the tree of the
> knowledge of good and evil you shall not eat, for in the day
> that you eat of it you shall surely die." (Gen. 2:16–17)

Notice this. The *first* command is *not* the prohibition. The
first command is the endorsement: "You may surely eat of every
tree." God essentially says to Adam, "Look at these trees. Beautiful, aren't they? That's why I gave you eyes—to see such beauty
in my world. Wait until you taste them. They will blow you
away. That's why I gave you a tongue—to taste and see the
goodness of my bounty. You may eat from every one of them.
All of them are yours for food. Except one. There is one no in
this world full of yes! Eat, drink, and be merry!"

Taking this enthusiastic exhortation as a model, here we see
the divine endorsement of *sensible pleasures*, that is, things that
we enjoy through our bodily senses. Things we see—the brilliant
purples, reds, and oranges of a sunset; the diamond blanket of
stars arrayed every night; the panoramic glory of a fertile valley
seen from the top of a mountain; the majesty of a well-cultivated
garden in early summer. Things we hear—the steady crashing
of waves on a shoreline; the songs of birds in early spring after
the long silence of winter; the soul-stirring harmony of strings,
woodwinds, brass, and percussion; the innocent refreshment
of the laughter of children. Things we smell—the fragrance of
roses, the aroma of pine, the delightful odor of cedar, the scent
of a home-cooked meal. Things we taste—the warm sweetness
of chocolate chip cookies, the puckering sour of a glass of lemonade, the heavenly savoriness of a plate piled high with bacon,

the surprising yet delightful bitterness of herbs, the piercing saltiness of well-seasoned meat. And things we touch—the cool smoothness of cotton bedsheets, the warm comfort of a wool blanket, the reassuring strength of a hug from a friend, the soft tenderness of a kiss from your spouse. All of these are gifts from God for our enjoyment. Yes, there are boundaries. There are limits to how and when and in what way we may enjoy the gifts of God. But as with Adam in the garden, these boundaries serve our joy. Just as the walls around a city are designed to preserve and enable life to happen inside, so the divine no's are designed to encourage and enable the deep and lasting enjoyment of his yes!

RELATIONAL PLEASURES—PEOPLE WE LOVE

Second, not only does God endorse our enjoyment of sensible pleasures; he also lavishly supplies us with *relational pleasures*. Consider the story in Genesis 2:18–25.

> Then the LORD God said, "It is not good that the man should be alone; I will make him a helper fit for him." (v. 18)

Five and a half days of "God saw that it was good." Now, in the middle of day six, "Not good." God sees something missing in his image bearer, some gap that must be filled. But before filling that gap, he takes Adam on a journey of growth and maturity, as he brings the animals to Adam for him to name them (Gen. 2:19–20). Through this exercise in naming, Adam comes to know not only the animals and the world around him but also himself. In seeing the pairs of cattle and canines and camels and cats, Adam comes to recognize that something is missing for him. He lacks a helper *fit* for him. Elephants may be impressive, but they aren't a good fit. Bunnies are cute but make lousy companions. A dog may be man's best friend, but God will not rest until he's exceeded loyalty and slobber. And because no suitable helper can be found among the living creatures, God resolves to build one from Adam himself.

> So the LORD God caused a deep sleep to fall upon the man, and while he slept took one of his ribs and closed up its place with flesh. And the rib that the LORD God had taken from the man he made into a woman and brought her to the man. (Gen. 2:21–22)

God puts Adam into a deep, death-like sleep. And while in that sleep, Adam loses something, a rib from his side. But he wakes to the stunning reality that he has not lost anything at all. This is better. This is fitting. This exceeds all expectations. Being raised up, he has moved from one degree of glory to another.

And the glory of woman's creation is not lost on Adam. Genesis 2:23 contains the first recorded *human* words in the Scriptures. Adam had previously named the animals and had likely conversed with God. But we have not heard his voice until now:

> This at last is bone of my bones
>> and flesh of my flesh;
> she shall be called Woman,
>> because she was taken out of Man. (Gen. 2:23)

Adam is a poet, and his first recorded words are a poem, an encomium, a hymn of praise—*the object of which is another creature*. We must let the significance of this event land on us. Adam beholds this helper, this other, this being who is like him but not him, and out of the overflow of his heart, his mouth speaks. He gazes on his bride in all her glory and without a shred of idolatry composes an ode *to her*:

41

You come from me, but you are not me. Your bones were built from my bones. Your flesh was cut from my flesh. We are alike but different. We are the same but sundered. God has torn me in two, only to put me together again. He removed from me a rib so that he might return it with interest. He has divided me from myself so that solitary unity might give way to complementary union. What name will express this? I am Adam, formed by Yahweh from the ground [Heb. *adamah*]. You then shall be Woman [Heb. *ishshah*] because you were taken out of Man [Heb. *ish*].

Adam's triumphant "At last!" signals to us that he is receiving the gift of relational pleasure. For us, Eve represents all the people we love. The father whose laughter stabilizes the soul. The mother whose tenderness comforts our affliction. The husband whose strength and provision support a household. The wife whose diligence and wisdom astound the world. The son whose curiosity awakens wonder in those around him. The daughter whose innocence leaves us speechless. The brother whose loyalty steels us in adversity. The sister whose grace and compassion move us to tears. And all the friends and mentors and counselors and people who extend these bonds beyond the limits of blood and kinship.

It is not good for us to be alone. And as with Adam, it would be foolish for us to say to God, "What do you mean 'alone'? I have you, God." That is true, and beside the point. God has made us to need people, to love people, to delight in people. Human isolation is a problem, a defect, and God acts to overcome the lack. Note this: *God* acts. *God* meets the need. *God* gives us life and breath and everything. And he has designed us so that *he* will meet some of our needs *through other people.*

VOCATIONAL PLEASURES—ACTIVITIES WE DO

The final category of pleasures from Genesis 1 and 2 is the context for all the other joys. God gives Adam and Eve a mission. He places them in the garden "to work it and keep it" (Gen. 2:15). They are to guard and protect the sacred space of the garden, just as the priests will later guard and protect the sacred space of the temple. But not only are they called to *guard* sacred space; God calls his image bearers to *extend* sacred space. They are to be fruitful, multiply, and fill the earth. More than that, they are to subdue the earth and exercise dominion over it as kings and queens under the high king of heaven. And, finally, as we've already seen, God enlists Adam and Eve in naming his world, in drawing out the meaning and implications of what God has done, and, like the prophets, shaping the future by their very words.

This calling—to represent God as his image bearers by working and guarding and multiplying and filling and subduing and reigning and naming and speaking—is the source of all our *vocational pleasures*. All the legitimate and honorable activities we delight to do as human beings are given to us by God. From cooking a delicious meal to building a sturdy house. From growing a garden to painting a portrait. From studying the movements of electrons to coaching a youth soccer team. From streamlining the shipment of goods across the country to preaching the word of God on the Lord's Day. As human beings, we were made to extend God's reign by using our minds and our bodies in fruitful and productive labor for the good of other people and the glory of God.

Not only are vocational pleasures enjoyable in themselves, but they are also the context for many of our other joys. Sensible and relational pleasures weren't given to us just for our enjoyment; they are also provision for God's mission. Food doesn't simply delight our tongues; it strengthens our bodies so that we can labor unto the Lord. Eve is a delight to Adam, yes. But she is also necessary to fulfill the mission to be fruitful and multiply. Adam cannot fill the earth all by his lonesome. God's mission demands the fruitfulness of men and women in producing godly offspring to image God around the world. And extending this point, God has given all of us friends, family, and neighbors so that we might stir one another up to love and good deeds and aid one another in filling the earth with the glory of God as the waters cover the sea.

Conclusion

This then is the point. What does supreme and full and expanding love for God look like when it meets one of his gifts? Glad reception and enjoyment of his gifts. In his original righteousness, Adam loved God fully and supremely and expansively, and, as a result, he ate his food with a glad and grateful heart. He celebrated his bride with a full and happy soul. He received his mission with eagerness and expectation at what God would do in him and through him.

And so it is with us. Glad enjoyment of fish tacos is what supreme love for God looks like when it eats fish tacos. Delight in and care for your neighbor is what supreme and full and expanding love for God looks like when it encounters your neighbor. And eager and expectant labor in the Lord is what supreme and full and expanding love for God looks like when we are given a task and a mission.

The banner over God's design in Genesis 1 and 2 is given to us in Genesis 1:31: "God saw everything that he had made, and behold, it was very good." Creatureliness, sensible pleasures, relational pleasures, vocational pleasures—according to Genesis 1 and 2 all these are very good, and this goodness persists after the fall. The taste of honey is still sweet. The way of a man with a woman is still a wonder and a delight and a great mystery. And our labor, even after the curse, is still a good gift from a loving Father. God created a world of yes, because he is fundamentally a God of yes, a giver who delights to give good things to his children.

3

Enjoying the Gifts When
Jesus Is Better

Up to this point, I've been emphasizing that God's world shows us what he's like and invites us to know him and enjoy him. General revelation in nature and culture and special revelation in the Scriptures work together so that we have experiential categories for knowing and loving God. The pleasures of this world—whether sensible, relational, or vocational—are given to us by God for our enjoyment and as a means of accomplishing his mission in the world. With these two truths in place, we're now ready to revisit the biblical tension we identified in the introduction. How do we resolve the tension created by the Totalizing passages and the Things of Earth passages, and then how does resolving the biblical tension help us with the experiential tension—the low-grade guilt and reluctant enjoyment in our daily lives?

Let's begin with a simple paradigm for understanding those passages. My suggestion is that the Bible gives us two complementary ways of approaching God and his gifts. The first is a comparative approach, in which God and his gifts are separated and set next to each other to determine which is more valuable. Put God on one side of the scales and his gifts and pleasures on the other and ask, "Which is greater? Which is more precious?" And if they're separated in that way, then the only right answer is that God has all value, and creation is dust on the scales. In himself, God is infinitely all-sufficient, glorious, and all-satisfying so that we say, "There is nothing I desire beside you. I count everything as loss compared to the surpassing worth of knowing Jesus Christ. Next to him, everything is rubbish." That's the comparative approach.

The second, I call the integrated approach, in which God and his gifts are enjoyed together so that we don't separate them or treat them as rivals. Instead, in the words of Charles Simeon, we "enjoy God in everything and everything in God." We attempt to receive the gifts of God in the way Adam did in the garden. Adam loved God fully and supremely and increasingly, and he still ate from those trees, and he still cried out, "At last!" when God brought Eve to him, and he still received the call to work and guard and subdue with a glad and grateful heart.

The integrated approach is built on the truth that we explored in the first chapter—namely, that God's gifts can serve our love for him by creating mental categories and emotional frameworks for engaging and delighting in God himself. Because God's goodness is *really* present in his gifts, we are free to enjoy *them* deeply for *his* sake. God's gifts become avenues for enjoying him, beams of glory that we chase back to the source. The paradigm passage for me is Proverbs 24:13–14:

> My son, eat honey, for it is good,
>> and the drippings of the honeycomb are sweet to your
>>> taste.
> Know that wisdom is such to your soul.

Why did God make honey so tasty and sweet? So that we would have some idea what wisdom is like (at least, that's one reason). The sweetness of honey points beyond itself to the wisdom of God. Honey is "good," and we are exhorted in Psalm 34 to "taste and see that *the* LORD is good!" (v. 8). In other words, our souls have taste buds, just like our tongues, and we can train the soul buds by exercising the tongue buds. We savor the sweetness of honey (or sweet tea or pumpkin crunch cake) as a means of creating new categories for our enjoyment of God and his wisdom. As we saw in the first chapter, honey declares the glory of God, and it does so directly. There is a straight line between the goodness and sweetness of honey and the goodness and sweetness of God. We use our senses and our minds to connect the physical enjoyment of honey to our souls and say, "God is like this. He's more than this. But he is like this."

At a practical level, this means that we can't short-circuit our enjoyment of honey. There's no shortcut or work-around. Think of it this way: there are two exhortations in Proverbs 24:13–14: (1) eat honey, and (2) know that wisdom is such to your soul. You can't obey the second until you've obeyed the first. Or to put it positively, in order for us to gain the full *spiritual* benefit of honey, we must *first* enjoy its sweetness. There must be a savoring of honey *as honey* before there can ever be a savoring of honey as a pointer to divine wisdom and glory. In short, if we are to obey the biblical exhortation to "*know* that wisdom is *such* to your soul," we must first "eat honey, for it is good."

A moment ago I called Proverbs 24:13–14 a "paradigm passage." By that, I mean that honey is a representative example of how to enjoy the things of earth for the glory of God. As C. S. Lewis once noted, every pleasure has the capacity to be a tiny theophany, a little revelation of God. Every bush is a burning bush, if only we have eyes to see. In other words, in principle, everything God has made is an invitation to know him more deeply. The heavens, the birds of the air, the lilies of the field, the wide-eyed wonder of children, a sirloin steak cooked just right, the sweetness of your wife's voice on the phone while you're away on a trip—all of these are invitations from God to come further up and further in. He's calling us to plunge headlong into the ocean of his gifts and then, as we come up for air, to sing like we've never sung before. By deeply enjoying the world God has made, we are able to love him with expanded minds and enlarged hearts and increased strength.

But as we do, we must be mindful of two dangers. On the one hand, because God intends for us to know him and understand him and to grow in knowledge of him through the natural world, it would be wrong and sinful of us to ignore the natural world. If God is speaking through the heavens and the birds and the lilies and the sun and the honey, then how closely are we listening? Are we awake to reality? Or have we been lulled to sleep? Have we become numb to the glory around us? Psalm 111:2 tells us, "Great are the works of the LORD, studied by all who delight in them." That's our aim. We want to delight in the works of the Lord, and out of that delight, to study, to focus, to think, to dig, to get into the tall grass and understand this amazing world that God has made. Or, to put it in terms of Proverbs 24, we're not going to try to know wisdom *apart from* eating honey.

But the second danger runs in the other direction. If *God* is revealing himself in and through the natural world, then it's not enough for us to attend to creation; we must also attend to him. These are the works *of the Lord* that we are delighting in and studying. In the same way that we can't seek to know God apart from his works, so also we can't treat his works as ends in themselves. It's not enough for us to simply eat honey because it's good. There's another step, and that other step must happen, or we're missing it. We must devote careful attention to the world God made, and then we must follow the rivers back to the source. We must chase the sunbeams back to the sun.

So then, there is the comparative approach—separate God from his gifts and ask which is more valuable and worthy. And there is the integrated approach—enjoy God in everything and everything in God. The next question is a practical one: What do we do with these two approaches? How do we relate them to each other? My suggestion, based on the way they are used in the Scriptures, is that we should seek to live integrated lives—enjoying God in everything and everything in God—and we should use the comparative approach as a series of tests to ensure that our integration doesn't become idolatry.

Idolatry and Ingratitude

So let's briefly explore what the Bible says about idolatry. Romans 1 is the classic passage on the subject. Paul tells us that creation reveals who God is and what he is like (Rom. 1:19–20). God's invisible attributes—his eternity, his power, his character, his beauty—are clearly seen in the things that have been made. They are evident and obvious in creation. As we saw in the first chapter, made things make invisible attributes visible. Honey and sunsets, rainstorms and day lilies, elm trees and infants—all these reveal what God is like and invite us to know and delight in him.

But this isn't the whole story. Because of the fall, we all enter the world broken and sinful. Because of our sinfulness, something goes wrong with this revelation and communication from God. One way to put it is that we suppress the truth in unrighteousness (1:18). We receive the communication and then pretend that we hear nothing. We press it down until we even convince ourselves that we aren't hearing it, even though it has been clearly sounding ever since the creation of the world. Or, to put it another way, we refuse to honor God as God and give thanks (1:21). These are the two fundamental sins that human beings commit: idolatry and ingratitude. God is unbelievably, incredibly kind and good to us, lavishing us with good things, big and small. And in our unrighteousness we do two things: we refuse to acknowledge that he is God, the source of all truth and goodness and beauty, and we refuse to say thank you for his many gifts. In our ungodliness, we won't admit that God is the center and origin of everything, the joy of every joy, the pleasure at the heart of every pleasure.

Instead, Paul says, we engage in a series of trades, of dark exchanges. Remember the set of scales from earlier in the chapter? In Romans 1 we separate the gifts from the giver, *and we choose the gifts over the giver*. Instead of saying thank you, we turn the gifts into gods. We have the glory of the immortal God, but instead of receiving it in the things God has made, we exchange it for images of created things (Rom. 1:23). We have the truth about God, but instead of celebrating it, we suppress it and then exchange it for a lie, and we worship and serve things of earth rather than the maker of heaven and earth (Rom. 1:25).

Idolatry, then, is the separation of the gifts from the giver and then a preference for the gifts over the giver. We separate, and then we elevate. We exalt created things, including ourselves, above God. God's gifts ought to be avenues for enjoying him, beams we follow back to the sun. Instead, we make them into his rivals, rejecting him in favor of them.

This is one of the reasons those comparative passages are in the Bible. We are all prone to wander, even as Christians.

We are prone to forget the giver and fixate solely on the gift. So God gives us comparative passages to test our enjoyment of the things of earth. We are meant to live integrated lives, enjoying God in everything and everything in God. But because we are sinners, because the impulse to suppress the truth and exchange the glory still lurks in our hearts, God graciously tests our affections for him. God gives us the temporary separation of comparative passages and invites us to pray them and sing them and celebrate them and live them out through self-denial and sacrifice and suffering so that we avoid the permanent and suicidal separation of idolatry and ingratitude.

Jesus Is Better

And now perhaps you can see how these two approaches to God and his gifts help to redirect the experiential tension that I described in the introduction. These two approaches help us to respond rightly to those totalizing passages that teach that God is better than all earthly things, passages such as these:

> A day in your courts is better
>   than a thousand elsewhere. (Ps. 84:10)

> I have suffered the loss of all things and count them as rubbish, in order that I may gain Christ. (Phil. 3:8)

> Your steadfast love is better than life. (Ps. 63:3)

> You have put more joy in my heart
>   than they have when their grain and wine abound.
>   (Ps. 4:7)

Now, here's the question: What do we do with these truths? What effect do they have on our lives? Let's use a simple example, like pumpkin crunch cake, an autumn delight that my wife makes for me. What do I do with the truth that Jesus is better than pumpkin crunch cake? There are two possibilities. The first says, "I love pumpkin crunch cake. But Jesus is better. So maybe I shouldn't love the sweet pumpkin filling and the crispy cake topping and the crunchy pecans scattered throughout so much. Perhaps I should even mix in a little vinegar to spoil the taste. Maybe I should suppress my satisfaction in the cake so that it doesn't compete with my satisfaction in God." The second says, "This cake is unbelievably good, and it's just a fleeting taste of the fullness of joy that Jesus offers. As I eat it, I want to do so in such a way that I also taste and see that the Lord is good."

Do you see the difference? In the first case, we seek to make Jesus better by making creation worse. In the second, we seek to let creation be grand, only to remind ourselves that we have not yet begun to experience true grandeur. In the first, we try to make the cake dim so that Jesus shines brighter. In the second, we simply let the cake be itself, in all of its creamy and crunchy goodness, and discover that in the light of his face, the things of earth grow strangely *bright*. In the first, we make creation stoop so that Jesus stands taller. In the second, we let creation rise to its full height, reaching for the skies with all its towering pleasures, only to then confess from the low-down bottom of our heart that eye has not seen, ear has not heard, the heart of man has not imagined what God has prepared for those who love him (see 1 Cor. 2:9).

Jesus is better. The mountains of God's glory extend far beyond our present experience. These are but the fringes of his ways.

That's what we see in Psalm 4:7, isn't it? "You have put more joy in my heart than they have when their grain and wine abound." How shall we confess this meaningfully, if the grain and wine have never put any joy in our hearts whatsoever? How shall we say that his love is better than life if we refuse to enjoy life at all? To say that we desire nothing besides him is an empty compliment if it is *literally* true. It would be as if to say, "I desire nothing besides you because I've never desired anything at all." But surely what the psalmist means is, "I have desired many things in my life, many things of earth. But compared to you, they are as nothing. You are my strength. You are my portion. Jesus is better."

I want to conclude this chapter with a very simple and practical exhortation, because what we do with the undeniable truth that Jesus is better makes a huge practical difference. My main counsel to those struggling with how to enjoy the things of earth while knowing that Jesus is better would be to avoid suppressing any of their legitimate pleasures when they arise. Now, there are all kinds of qualifications I want to make about that advice. That's why there are chapters in this book about self-denial and generosity and suffering. Yes, we must test our delight in the things of earth by restraining our appetites and sacrificing good things in the cause of love. But we mustn't become permanent test takers who seek to somehow honor the giver by *refusing* to enjoy his gifts (or by enjoying them with low-grade guilt hanging over us like the plague). And, of course, it's important to stress that we're only talking about *legitimate* pleasures. Enjoying sinful pleasures is always out of bounds. Sinful desires and pleasures must be mortified, killed, put to death.

But when we're talking about legitimate earthly pleasures, my counsel is to take the governor off. If your joy in your family is going to shoot through the roof, don't reinforce the ceiling with steel. Perhaps even open the skylight so that it has a clearer shot. The reason is simple. If I am relating to God properly (and I realize that for many, this is a very big *if*), that is, if I know in my bones that Christ is the Alpha and Omega of all joy and delight, then I need not fear the lesser pleasures. Let them erupt. Let them soar as high as they can. For when they do, they carry my joy in God with them.

We don't test our faithfulness to Psalm 4 by throwing dull parties. Instead, we seek to have the best party possible and at the end of the night and in the midst of our joy, say, "This, even this, is but a picture and foretaste. Eye has not seen what God has for us." So don't throw out the grain and new wine; instead, gather in the sheaves and the grapes, add the fatted calf and the pumpkin crunch cake, and teach the world what feasting really is. And do so knowing that when we ourselves are one day reaped and gathered into barns, the mountains will flow with wine and the Son of Man himself, eyes twinkling with the joy set before him, will offer us the cup.

4

Anchor Points

In the last chapter, I argued that we resolve the biblical tension between Totalizing passages and Things of Earth passages by recognizing the comparative approach and the integrated approach as two complementary ways to view God and his gifts. I also argued that we ought to seek to live integrated lives—enjoying God in everything and everything in God—while using the Totalizing passages as comparative tests so that our integration doesn't become idolatry. The next three chapters will explore the ways that these two approaches work out in practice by weaving the comparative tests and the integrated life together.

I ended the last chapter with a practical exhortation to take the governor off our enjoyment of legitimate things of earth. However, some readers might wonder whether this is really wise. They might ask how such an exhortation is compatible with Colossians 3:1–4:

> If then you have been raised with Christ, seek the things that are above, where Christ is, seated at the right hand of God.

Set your minds on things that are above, not on things that are on earth. For you have died, and your life is hidden with Christ in God. When Christ who is your life appears, then you also will appear with him in glory.

This passage seems to run in the opposite direction of this book. Paul tells us *not* to set our minds on the things of earth. Instead, we're to set our minds on things above. High things. Holy things. *Not* earthly things. Can we reconcile Paul's exhortation and my exhortations in the previous chapters? I think we can. To do so, we need to ask two questions:

1. What does Paul mean by the "things that are on earth"?
2. What does Paul mean by "set your mind"?

Earthly Things

When Paul refers to the things on the earth, does he mean things like baseball, bacon cheeseburgers, game nights with the family, Shakespeare, working out, *Star Wars*, home repairs, and church picnics on sunny spring days? Is Paul telling us that we shouldn't seek those things at all or set our mind upon them in any sense? This is where careful reading of the passage can help. Look at the next verses. "Put to death therefore what is earthly in you: sexual immorality, impurity, passion, evil desire, and covetousness, which is idolatry. On account of these the wrath of God is coming" (Col. 3:5–6).

Now, the word for "earthly" in Colossians 3:5 and the word for the "things that are on earth" in Colossians 3:2 is the same word. So in the immediate context, earthly things doesn't mean "created things" but instead means something like "sinful things"—sinful behaviors, desires, and activities. It is these things that we are to reject in favor of the heavenly things, the things above.

We get confirmation of this interpretation when we try to answer the second question. What does Paul mean by "set your mind on"? This word shows up in a number of other places in Paul's writings. In Romans 8 there is a mind that is set on the Spirit (which is life and peace), and there is a mind that is set on the flesh (which is death). But it's in his letter to the Philippians that we get the most clarity. Consider two passages, the first one from chapter 3:

> For many, of whom I have often told you and now tell you even with tears, walk as enemies of the cross of Christ. Their end is destruction, their god is their belly, and they glory in their shame, with minds set on earthly things. (vv. 18–19)

That sounds remarkably similar to Colossians 3. The enemies of Christ's cross will be destroyed, just as those who indulge in sinful practices will endure the wrath of God. Christ's enemies make their belly into their god, just as some indulge covetousness, which is idolatry. And, of course, both passages mention people whose minds are set on earthly things. Now consider the second passage, Philippians 4:8:

> Finally, brothers, whatever is true, whatever is honorable, whatever is just, whatever is pure, whatever is lovely, whatever is commendable, if there is any excellence, if there is anything worthy of praise, think about these things.

The Greek word for "think" in this passage (*logizomai*) is different from the word for "setting your mind on" in the other passages (*phroneo*). And if we reflect upon the difference between them, a picture begins to emerge. Paul is saying that all of us have a fundamental orientation of the heart, what he calls a mind-set. That mind-set and orientation ought to be governed by the things above, where Christ is. If we orient our lives by earthly things, we commit idolatry, leading to wrath and destruction. But if we orient our lives by Christ, then we're free to think, to consider, to attend to *whatever* is true, good, and beautiful wherever we find it, whether in heaven or on earth. To put it succinctly, we *set our minds* on things above and then *consider* what is good and lovely in things below.

In other words, Paul is calling us to a life centered on Christ, rooted and grounded in God's love, and oriented by the glory and majesty and beauty of God. Because we've died with Christ, because our life is now hidden with him (Col. 3:3), therefore we must fix the fundamental direction of our minds and hearts on him always.

But we have to define *always* the way the Bible does. And this is where we often go wrong. We adopt a narrow and truncated picture of the mind that is set on things above. We think that a heavenly mind-set means we only do spiritual activities such as prayer and Bible reading. But if we look at Paul's description of the faithful Christian life in the rest of Colossians 3, we'll see just how earthy the heavenly mind-set is:

> Put on humility and meekness like a new robe (3:12); be patient and forgive each other (3:13); wear your love on your sleeve and watch it compose a symphony (3:14); put peace on the throne of your heart; and be thankful (3:15). Make the Scriptures at home in your soul. Teach and sing them to each other with thankfulness in your heart (3:16); do everything in the name of Jesus. And did I mention give thanks to God (3:17)?

> Wives, submit to your husbands (3:18); husbands, love your wives (3:19). Children, obey your parents; it makes God

happy (3:20). Fathers, don't provoke your children; that doesn't make God happy (3:21).

Are you under authority? Then obey those over you sincerely because you fear God (3:22). Do your work with gusto, because God will reward you (3:23–24). Are you in authority? Then be just and fair to those in your care, because you have a boss in heaven (4:1). Pray without ceasing. And, seriously, did I mention be grateful (4:2)? Pray that the missionaries would be fruitful and bold (4:3–4). Show the world how the wise walk by taking time away from the devil (4:5). Use salty language, the kind that gives grace (4:6).

According to Paul, the heavenly mind-set spends a lot of time thinking about and engaging with things on the earth. Family, neighbors, church, job, earthly joys—the person whose mind-set is governed by heavenly things intentionally and deliberately considers and engages them. The heavenly mind-set is profoundly earthy, but it is fundamentally oriented by the risen Christ.

And I like that word *orient* a lot. It implies that love for God guides and governs all our other thoughts, desires, and actions. Christ is the North Star, the fixed point that helps us to navigate our ship through life. To be oriented by the glory of Christ means, first, that Christ is the *supreme object* of our desire. To use Paul's language in Colossians, Christ *is* our life (3:4). Or as he says in Philippians 1:21, "For to me to live is Christ, and to die is gain." If Christ is your life, if living is Christ, that means that you view death, which is the loss of every good thing on earth, as gain, because you get more of Christ. He is your greatest treasure.

But orienting your life by Christ doesn't simply mean making him the supreme object of your desire; it also means making him the supreme *model* for your desires. When our minds are set on Christ, on the things above, then all our other desires are ordered properly. It's not just that we love him; it's that we love everything else that we love *in him*. Which means we love them in the way that he wants us to love them. In other words, setting your mind on things above means that you love God *and* that you love what God loves, that you supremely desire God *and* rightly desire everything that God desires.

That's what I think is implied in Colossians 3:5. What keeps the good desire for sex from degenerating into immorality, impurity, passion, and evil desire? Loving sex in the way that Christ wants us to love sex, within the boundaries that God has set in creation. What keeps a good desire for created things from falling into covetousness and idolatry? Loving created things in the way that God loves them, no more and no less. In other words, we take our cues from him so that he sets the boundaries and the contexts for our enjoyment of sex or creation or culture or whatever. He becomes the sun at the center of our solar system that makes all the planets orbit properly.

A Life Oriented by Christ

Now let's get practical by drawing together a few threads from this chapter and the ones before it. Begin with the fundamental truth that creation shows us what God is like. His invisible attributes are clearly perceived in the things that have been made. Now follow this basic logic.

1. Made things make invisible attributes visible.
2. You are a made thing.
3. Therefore, you make invisible attributes visible.

You are a word from God. God means something *through you.* You are communication from God about God, just like the heavens. Your conduct, your life, is itself a kind of divine speech. It is revelation from God, designed by him to show the world what he is like. Here's how this basic truth challenges me personally: Will I tell the truth about God or will I lie? Will God teach others about himself through me by way of comparison or by way of contrast? Everyone is going to glorify God one way or another. Either God will point at us and say, "I am something like that. That, even with all the flaws, is a little picture of what I'm like." Or he will point at us and say, "That's the opposite of what I'm like. I'm not that kind of husband. I'm not that kind of father. I'm not that kind of friend."

This is the fundamental choice that confronts us daily. Will we show the world what God is like in all our words and all our deeds? When you leave for work and when you come home from work? When you make dinner or clean up after dinner? When you have a fussy child or a frustrated spouse or a hurting friend? You are a made thing, and you were made to make invisible divine attributes visible to the world. As a husband, as a father, as a wife, as a mother, as a child, as a friend, as a pastor, you—your life, your speech, your conduct—ought to be a display of triune glory and an invitation to triune glory. You ought to be a testimony to grace and an invitation to grace. You should aim to be a walking, talking, living, breathing gospel proclamation.

How We Speak with Our Lives

At this point, the categories of general and special revelation that we explored in chapter 1 can help us. When I say that you are a word from God, and that therefore, in your actions, demeanor, attitude, and conduct, you ought to be proclaiming the gospel, I don't mean that you, as general revelation, are sufficient to save people. In other words, your smile to your children, your kindness to your coworker, or your patience with your friends, as a display of glory and an invitation to glory in itself will not save them from sin and death. Actual proclamation of the life, death, and resurrection of Jesus for sinners in words is essential for salvation. What I'm saying is that God created you and redeemed you so that your life, your attitude, your conduct, your patterns of speech would make the gospel more meaningful and comprehensible to others. That it would create categories in their hearts and minds that would light up when the grace of God lands in the verbal proclamation of the truth. This is the way that all revelation in creation works. It declares God's glory; it reveals his beauty and attributes; it even, I think, gives us images and pictures of the gospel, but in itself it is not the means of the new birth and conversion. Only the verbally proclaimed gospel is.

Having seen fourteen frigid Minnesota winters, I know that spring is coming. It's around the corner. And I know that God is preaching a resurrection sermon with every trip around the sun. Every fall, the world around me dies. And every spring, when the snow melts, when the buds return to the trees, when life blossoms all around me, it's as if I see a stone rolling away from the tomb. I see the same thing on a daily basis. I see the sun die every day as it plunges beneath the horizon in the west, and I see it come flying out of the grave in the east every morning, triumphantly dancing across the sky like a groom on his wedding day. General revelation preaches to me because I know the preached gospel. And that's what our lives ought to be.

A Made Thing That Makes Things

Second, not only are you a made thing, but you are a made thing that makes things. For the most part, we've been highlighting the fact that creation declares the glory of God—the heavens and the honey, the sunsets and the mountains. But as we saw in chapter 1 with the bread of life, human culture is also able to reveal the glory and perfections of God. Consider Psalm 84:10–11:

> For a day in your courts is better
>   than a thousand elsewhere.
> I would rather be a doorkeeper in the house of my God
>   than dwell in the tents of wickedness.
> For the LORD God is a sun and shield;
>   the LORD bestows favor and honor.
> No good thing does he withhold
>   from those who walk uprightly.

Notice the comparative approach in verse 10 (one day in God's presence is "better than" a thousand elsewhere). Notice how we can show what God is like by comparison or by contrast: we can be butlers in God's house, or lords in the tents of wickedness. Finally, notice both creation and culture showing us what God is like. God is a sun and shield. God made the sun. Humans made the shield. Both declare his glory. That's true of everything we do. It's why Paul tells us, "Whatever you do, work heartily, as for the Lord and not for men" (Col. 3:23). Whether you're working at Target to make sure the Cheerios end up on the shelves so people can eat, or managing a risk pool for a health insurer, or changing diapers and making a house into a home, or fixing bicycles so that people can ride to feel God's pleasure, or playing music and telling stories in order to move people's emotions, or investing in students so that they grow in knowledge and wisdom, or taking photographs to capture moments of beauty for people to enjoy, or helping people purchase a home or fixing a chimney or repairing the plumbing, or caring for the sick and injured. In all of these, we are made things that make things, and our aim in them must be to take the work of our hands, offer it to God, and say, "Establish this as a picture of who you are and what you're like."

Anchor Points

Finally, you are a made thing that needs anchor points. Anchor points establish rhythms of godwardness in our lives. Godwardness is the attempt to faithfully live out Paul's exhortation in 1 Corinthians 10:31: "Whether you eat or drink, or whatever you do, do all to the glory of God." But we can distinguish between two different types of godwardness, what I call "direct godwardness" and "indirect godwardness." Direct godwardness involves an intentional and direct focus on God himself. Prayer, worship, confession, reading the Bible—in all of these activities, we are attempting to engage with God directly. Indirect godwardness, on the other hand, involves a subtle and subconscious awareness of God's presence while actively and intentionally engaging in the world he has made. Eating a meal, playing softball, driving a car, mowing the lawn, writing an email, making love, having a conversation, reading a novel—in these activities, our attention is on the world around us. Our lives ought to be structured by regular rhythms of direct and indirect godwardness, moving back and forth between direct interaction with God himself and active engagement with the world. Up to God, out into the world. Up to God, out into the world. This is the rhythm of our lives. Let's consider a few examples.

Personal and family devotions, in which we read the word of God and seek his face in prayer—adoring him, confessing our sins, giving thanks, and making requests—anchor us on a daily basis. They are essential in cultivating a mind that is set on things above, because you cannot set your mind on things above if you never take time to actually direct your attention to things above—to Christ and the gospel and the glory of his appearing. A regular devotional life anchors us in the love of God and helps to order our desires and set godly boundaries on our affections for the things of the world. It helps to keep our love of created things from becoming idolatrous. In such times, we remind ourselves that we are hidden with Christ in God and that our future is secure, and this enables us to put to death the earthly passions that war against our soul. If you need help in cultivating a devotional life, I'd recommend the book *Habits of Grace* by my friend David Mathis.[4] It's an excellent one-stop shop for growing in your desire for Christ and the things above.

Or consider worshiping with God's people on the Lord's Day. This is corporate direct godwardness, as we worship God with his people. Or, more accurately, corporate worship is a mixture of direct and indirect godwardness as we set our minds on God himself but with a deep awareness of his people around us. We lift up our prayers to him, but we do so with the prayers of his people, both in the room and around the world. We raise our voices to him in song, but as we sing and make melody to him, we also address one another with psalms and hymns and spiritual songs (Eph. 5:19). Corporate godwardness is the anchor for our week. And it's absolutely essential. Biblical authors tell us that we must not neglect meeting together (Heb. 10:25) but instead to encourage one another and stir one another up to love and good deeds.

At my church, when we worship the living God on the Lord's Day, we always walk through the gospel in our five-step liturgy that involves a mixture of prayers, Scripture, and song (and which we summarize using five Cs). We begin with the *call* to worship, in which God through the pastor invites us into his presence. We then move to *confession*, as we corporately and personally repent of our sins. We then move to *consecration* through the preaching of the word, as God sets us apart for his service and renews our minds in conformity to his will. The sermon always lands at the Lord's Table, as we partake of the bread and wine together in *Communion*. And finally, we conclude with the *commission*, as God sends us out into the world with the mission to make disciples of all nations. We gather every week in the eager expectation that God will meet us, that we'll see the worth of Jesus, who is our life, and that sight will transform us from one degree of glory to another.

In the absence of corporate worship and personal devotions, we will inevitably anchor ourselves in something else. Our spiritual lives will drift. Yes, we can meet with God in nature—at the lake, in the deer stand, on the mountains. God is present everywhere. But these encounters with God in nature cannot replace encounters with God in his word and with his people. We must not neglect meeting together, as is the habit of some. Without corporate worship and personal prayer and reflection on the Scriptures, our engagement with God in nature is hollowed out. We begin to remake God in our own image. We begin to be anchored in our own private ideas of what God is like rather than the work of Christ and the revelation of God in the Scriptures.

It's not a question of whether we'll have our minds set on something. The question is what that something will be. Will it be Christ, or will it be our jobs, or television, or social media, or our families? All of these are good as planets in our solar system, but they are terrible as the sun. If we try to make them the sun, if we set our minds on them and seek them supremely, they fall apart and fail us and go wrong.

I regularly ask myself a series of questions to evaluate whether my direct godwardness is rightly orienting and anchoring my daily life:

1. How often does direct godwardness (however brief) spontaneously erupt? As I go about my day, do I find myself regularly going godward with prayers and supplications and requests and thanksgiving and adoration? Is God always in my field of vision so that no matter how intently I'm focusing on the task at hand, direct communion with him is never far away? Is he always present, even when he's not being addressed?

2. Is there an increasing awareness of God's presence in everything I do? In other words, is there a growing sense that I'm never far from God, that he is always close at hand, that he is always marking me and speaking to me and guiding me through life?

3. Do I find myself desiring to linger in prayer or song or Scripture reading? When life thrusts itself upon me again, and I must put down my Bible in order to make breakfast for the kids or head off to work, do I find myself wishing I had a few more minutes? More importantly, do I eagerly look forward to the next time that I can be alone with God? Do I look forward to the next time when I can worship God with his people?

4. Is the word of God fresh in my heart? Or is it a dead letter, a sign that I've been merely checking the devotional box on my to-do list?

5. Finally, and most importantly, is there fruit in my life? Am I making progress in holiness? Am I putting to death what is earthly in me? Can I see evidence of growth in godliness over the past six months, twelve months, two years? Not that there aren't still struggles or setbacks. But am I slowly and steadily becoming a more loving, joyful, caring, patient, thankful, and humble person? Does my life increasingly display the fruit of the Spirit?

Conclusion

All these efforts to actively orient our lives by Christ must flow from the fact that we have died with him and have now been raised with him and hidden in him. Our labors to fix our minds upon him must be rooted in the finished work of Christ. He is our Savior. He is our Lord. He is our treasure. He is our life. Our lives are thus marked by rhythms of godwardness as we seek him directly and indirectly. We pray and meditate on the Scriptures regularly, attentively, and with perseverance so that God is always the supreme object and the supreme model for our desires. Then we enter our days anchored in the gospel and rooted in the love of God with our hearts and minds tuned to his presence and reality in the things he has made. We seek to enter our daily tasks *alive*—to God, to the wonders of his world, and to the needs of others.

Throughout our day, wherever we are, we seek to be all there, fully present to the people around us and to the tasks at hand. We punctuate our day with moments of direct godwardness— before meals, during solitary commutes, in the midst of breaks in the action, before and after difficult tasks, and a thousand other possibilities. We orient our weeks by gathering with God's people in worship, collectively singing praises, confessing sins, hearing the word preached, and sharing fellowship at the Lord's

Table. Our worship on the Lord's Day leads us to an encounter with the grace of God in Christ, rooting us and grounding us in the love of God and the cross of Christ and then sending us out into the world as salt and light, ready to proclaim and portray the gospel in our words and works.

5

Denying Ourselves and Sharing Our Riches

We've seen that God reveals himself to us in his word and in his world. General revelation and special revelation work together to give us deep and rich knowledge of God. The heavens declare the glory of God. So do the birds of the air and the lilies of the field. All of creation reveals who God is and what he is like, and it does so through a woven web of images and metaphors and pictures and analogies. Made things make invisible attributes visible. God has given us our bodily senses in order to gain knowledge of the world, and he has given us minds and hearts in order to connect our experience of the world to the God who made it. We taste and see that honey is good as a way of creating categories in our experience so that we can taste and see that the Lord is good. The Bible is the grammar textbook for the language of God in creation, and by immersing ourselves in the Bible, we're able to rightly hear what God is saying everywhere else. Special revelation guards our interpretation of general revelation, and general revelation enriches our knowledge of special revelation.

We've also seen that God intentionally filled the world with all kinds of pleasures—sensible pleasures, relational pleasures, and vocational pleasures. He gives these good gifts to us both for our enjoyment and so that we can accomplish his mission in the world. With God as the supreme object of our desires and the supreme model for our desires, we are called to enjoy God in everything and everything in God. This is an integrated approach to God and his gifts. On the other hand, because of the very real dangers of idolatry and ingratitude, we also use comparative tests to remind ourselves that God is more satisfying than all of his gifts, that his steadfast love is better than life, that living is Christ and dying is gain. Jesus is always better. Practically, we live this out through rhythms of godwardness, as we anchor ourselves through personal devotions and corporate worship, and then live our lives conscious of God's presence and nearness. We too are made things, and in all that we say and do, we must show the world what God is like.

Now I'm very aware that encouraging people to plunge headlong into the ocean of God's gifts and deeply delight in the things of earth is dangerous. It would be easy to hear what I've said thus far and think that I'm preaching some kind of health, wealth, and prosperity gospel. You might take my words and use them to justify hoarding God's gifts for yourself, rationalizing your luxurious lifestyle and expensive purchases on the grounds that you just want to enjoy God in everything (especially the finer things in life). And this kind of mistake could be deadly to your soul. The love of money is the root of all kinds of evil. Those who desire to be rich fall into a snare. You can't serve God and mammon. These biblical warnings ring in our ears as we seek to rightly enjoy the things of earth. The present chapter explores two comparative tests that guard us from falling into covetousness, greed, and idolatry: self-denial and generosity.

Biblical Self-Denial

Biblical self-denial is the voluntary giving up of good things for the sake of better things. I'm stressing the word *biblical* in order to distinguish Christian self-denial from pagan asceticism. There is an undeniable and unavoidable strain of asceticism in the Scriptures. We can't ignore or minimize it. But we must recognize that Christian asceticism and self-denial has a particular and unique shape. There are five main characteristics of biblical self-denial. First, biblical self-denial, unlike other religious forms of self-denial, stresses the goodness of the gifts, even when we abstain from them. We start with Paul's conviction in 1 Timothy 4, that everything created by God is good, and nothing is to be rejected if it is received with thanksgiving (4:4). According to Paul, those who forbid marriage and require abstinence from foods (presumably because both marriage and food are tied closely to sensible pleasures) are propagating the teaching of demons (4:3). Instead, we ought to receive good things with gratitude, sanctifying them by the word of God and prayer (4:5). Or to use the language from the previous chapter, our enjoyment of marriage and food is marked by rhythms of godwardness—we sanctify God's gifts by setting them apart through our direct godwardness (word and prayer) and then enjoying them through our indirect godwardness (receiving them with thanksgiving).

Second, biblical self-denial recognizes the goodness of divine boundaries for our enjoyment of the gifts themselves. Self-restraint and self-control serve our joy in God's gifts. If you drown yourself in lemonade, you lose the true and proper enjoyment of lemonade. If you gorge yourself on pumpkin crunch cake, you lose the proper enjoyment of pumpkin crunch cake. Joy in God's gifts depends in part on what C. S. Lewis calls resisting the impulse of Encore, that itch to overly indulge our earthly appetites and to have things over again and again and again.[5] The lust for Encore attempts to treat a single good as though it were the only good. Instead of embracing the Solomonic truth that there is a time for everything, a season for every activity under the sun, we refuse other, different goods and pleasures in favor of the one that has enthralled us in the moment. We gorge ourselves on one good and reject the other goods that God intended for us. Rather than allow God to give us a symphony, we insist on playing the same note over and over and over again.

Biblical self-denial puts the lust for Encore to death and thereby opens us to the full spectrum of God's gifts. By restraining our earthly appetites, we make space for the distinct pleasures of anticipation and memory. Whether we're talking about a child eagerly awaiting Christmas morning or a married couple planning an anniversary trip, we all know that looking forward to some great event is itself pleasurable. What's more, we know that memories of past joys have a way of growing and maturing and sweetening with time. Again, as Lewis reminds us, a pleasure is only full grown when it is remembered.[6] Resisting Encore makes it possible for us to fully enjoy God's gifts through anticipation, through possession, and through reflection.

Third, not only does self-denial serve our joy in God's gifts, it also maximizes our joy in God himself. Self-denial includes activities such as fasting, in which we forgo food for a time in order to increase our hunger for God. We *deny* our earthly appetite in order to *increase* our earthly appetite ultimately so that we can connect our longing for food to our longing for God.

"This much, O God, I want you." Fasting serves our joy in God by reminding us that Jesus is the true bread that has come down from heaven to give life to the world. Jesus is better.

Fourth, through biblical self-denial not only do we restrain our normal, earthly appetites, and not only do we temporarily fast from food in order to increase our spiritual appetite, but we also willingly give up good things in order to follow Jesus on the Calvary road.

> If anyone would come after me, let him deny himself and take up his cross daily and follow me. For whoever would save his life will lose it, but whoever loses his life for my sake will save it. For what does it profit a man if he gains the whole world and loses or forfeits himself? (Luke 9:23–25)

There is a death and resurrection movement in all our self-denial. We lose our life in order to save it. We forfeit the world that we might gain ourselves. We willingly suffer daily death in order that we might, like Christ, be triumphantly raised from the dead.

In this way, self-denial guards us from worldliness. The apostle John exhorts Christians, "Do not love the world or the things in the world" (1 John 2:15). By "world," he means creation and culture as bent toward sin and ungodliness. The things in the world—the desires of the flesh, the desires of the eyes, and the pride of life—do not come to us directly from the Father but have been twisted and broken by sin. "The desires of the flesh" refers to bodily desires that have been corrupted and distorted by sin. "Desires of the eyes" refers to beautiful things that have become a spectacle to distract us from God. And the "pride of life" refers to all of the pomp, glory, and splendor of the world that we treasure and trust in instead of the Lord. That's why the love for the world and love for the Father are mutually exclusive.

To love the world is to so esteem and value it that we covetously desire and crave the things of the world. In the words of the last chapter, it's to set our minds upon and fix our hearts upon the things below so that we spend the vast majority of our energy, thought, and speech on acquiring more of the world's goods. In other words, to love the world is to fail the comparative test. Like those who were invited to the Lord's banquet in Luke 14, we hold our property, our wealth, and our families in higher esteem than the things of Christ. We prefer things below to things above. And we are condemned and cast out for it.

Self-denial keeps our legitimate love of earthly things in check. It keeps our desires in their proper place by giving up good things for the sake of better things. It shows that we hold all of our earthly goods with an open hand. We enjoy them when we have them. But we don't covet and crave them. We refuse to set our minds upon them. We can voluntarily give them up for the sake of knowing Christ Jesus our Lord.

Finally, biblical self-denial is always accompanied by "unblushing promises of reward," both in this life and the one to come. Consider Jesus's words to his disciples in Mark 10. The rich young ruler has just refused to leave his wealth in order to follow Christ. Jesus then warns of the dangers of wealth; it's hard for a rich man to enter the kingdom (10:23). After Jesus describes the impossibility of salvation apart from God, Peter says, "See, we have left everything and followed you" (10:28). In other words, Peter drew attention to the self-denial of the disciples. Jesus's response is incredible:

> Truly, I say to you, there is no one who has left house or
> brothers or sisters or mother or father or children or lands,

for my sake and for the gospel, who will not receive a hundredfold now in this time, houses and brothers and sisters and mothers and children and lands, with persecutions, and in the age to come eternal life. (10:29–30)

A few observations about Jesus's words. First, the self-denial is for Jesus's sake and the gospel. Second, those who deny themselves receive back things both "now in this time" and "in the age to come." Third, what they receive back in this time far surpasses what they give up ("a hundredfold"). Fourth, the glory of what they receive back now is not untouched by pain and hardship but still carries persecutions with it.

From this, I conclude that when we leave good things for the sake of Christ, God gives us back good things, with interest. The form that the returned gift takes may vary. You may give up your house for Christ, and he might return to you a better house (with "better" being defined by fruitfulness for you, your family, and the kingdom, not necessarily by size or expense). You may lose your family for the gospel, and God may restore familial fellowship through the church. The returned gift may simply be the manifest presence of God in your life in the midst of your losses. But whatever form the replacement gift takes, Jesus is clear—we ought to expect a hundredfold value returned to us in this life (even with continued suffering), and in the age to come, eternal life.

This is how biblical self-denial tests our integrated joy. We begin with the goodness of the gift that we give up. We restrain our earthly appetites and resist the urge of Encore so that we can enjoy the full array of earthly pleasures. We temporarily fast so that we can feast on God himself. We deny ourselves daily in order to follow Christ with a cross on our backs and avoid the snare of worldliness. And we do so in order to receive a hundredfold reward from God in the present age and in the age to come, eternal life.

Generosity

Self-denial is not the only comparative test for our enjoyment of the things of earth. Generosity takes self-denial to another level. Generosity is not just a giving *up*; it's a giving *to*. It's the voluntary giving of good things to others in the cause of love. My favorite passage on this subject is 1 Timothy 6:17–19:

> As for the rich in this present age, charge them not to be haughty, nor to set their hopes on the uncertainty of riches, but on God, who richly provides us with everything to enjoy. They are to do good, to be rich in good works, to be generous and ready to share, thus storing up treasure for themselves as a good foundation for the future, so that they may take hold of that which is truly life.

Notice first that Paul's exhortation is to the rich. If you're reading this book, you're likely included in this category. Compared to 99 percent of the people in history, every one of us is wealthy. Houses, iPhones, blue jeans, minivans, central air-conditioning, central plumbing, trips to Disney World, access to medical care, Chinese food, comfortable tennis shoes. We are unfathomably wealthy, which means that Paul is speaking directly to us here.

And what does he say? He gives us three exhortations in this passage. First, don't be haughty. It's easy for the rich to think that they're somebody, to boast in their riches. It's easy for the rich to think, "My right arm has gotten me this wealth." It's easy to live as though life consists in an abundance of possessions, that if we can just get the big house or the big car or the big vacation, then other people will admire us and respect us. Wealth and haughtiness often go hand in hand. There's a smug satisfaction that creeps in and lords our riches over others. So Paul's first word to the rich is, "Don't boast! Don't puff yourself up in your riches."

The second exhortation is similar: Don't set your hope on the uncertainty of riches. It's easy for wealthy people to think that their strength comes from their wealth and not from Christ. We so easily modify Paul's famous words in Philippians 4:13: "I can do all things through *wealth* which strengthens me." It's easy to forget Paul's words earlier in 1 Timothy 6:

> But godliness with contentment is great gain, for we brought nothing into the world, and we cannot take anything out of the world. But if we have food and clothing, with these we will be content. But those who desire to be rich fall into temptation, into a snare, into many senseless and harmful desires that plunge people into ruin and destruction. For the love of money is a root of all kinds of evils. It is through this craving that some have wandered away from the faith and pierced themselves with many pangs. (vv. 6–10)

Our riches are uncertain because we can't take them with us. All the wealth in the world won't keep us from dying. It's not wrong to be rich, but, Paul says, to *desire* to be rich, to love money, to crave wealth is a deep temptation, a snare, and all kinds of evil flow from it. The love of money will ruin you. The craving for riches will destroy you. Desiring to be rich jeopardizes your faith. Therefore, to the rich in this present age, Paul says, "Don't set your hope on your riches."

Instead (and this is the third exhortation), set your hope on God. Don't set your hope on riches; set your hope on God. He's not uncertain. He's not unstable. Moth and rust don't destroy him; thieves cannot steal him from you. You can take God with you out of this world. He will never leave you nor forsake you. The love of God is the root of all sorts of goodness, and to crave him and to desire him brings the deepest and most lasting joy. In his presence is fullness of joy; at his right hand are pleasures forevermore.

Now up to this point, Paul is making a lot of sense. If you're rich, don't boast; don't set your hope on your riches; set your hope on God. But now, at the end of 1 Timothy 6:17, he surprises us. He reminds the rich that God "richly provides us with everything to enjoy." Personally, that's not what I would expect Paul to say to the rich. Nonetheless, Paul tells Timothy to remind the rich in this present age that God has given them their wealth so that they would enjoy it. So the question becomes, how do you enjoy everything that God richly provides *without* setting your hope on the uncertainty of riches? I think that the rest of the passage shows us how. Paul here gives us an important test to ensure that we enjoy God's provision without setting our hope upon it.

Notice the flow of the passage: set your hope on God, set your mind on things above, orient your life by the gospel of Jesus, and while you do, remember that he richly provides you with everything, and he has purposes for his provision. And there are four purposes (not just one):

1. To enjoy
2. To do good
3. To be rich in good works
4. To be generous and ready to share

How do we test whether we're enjoying God's gifts rightly? By our generosity. By our eagerness to do good. By whether we are as rich in good works as we are in money. If wealth comes to us and we're enjoying it, but it's not spilling the banks and flooding the lives of others, then something has gone wrong in our souls.

This is the same movement that we saw in Genesis 1 and 2. God gave Adam all manner of gifts for his enjoyment—tasty food, a loving wife, and fruitful labor. But he also gave him these gifts for the sake of God's mission to fill the earth with his glory. Gifts are given for our enjoyment, and gifts are given for God's mission. When we consider this movement in light of the rest of the book, the following picture emerges. We receive the gift. We enjoy it with thanksgiving, acknowledging that God is the one who gives it to us. This thanksgiving spills over into worship, since we know that as good as the gift is, it's just a taste of his goodness. And then satisfied with God and enjoying his provision, our lives become a tidal wave of generosity—eager to do good, on the lookout for needs and ready with open-handed and big-hearted generosity. Our goal is this: we want to be as generous with others as God has been with us. We want to freely receive because he richly provides us with everything to enjoy, and therefore freely give because he richly provides us with everything to share.

Now, I can't tell you precisely how much to give. The Old Testament required a tithe. Jesus told the rich young ruler to sell everything he had (Luke 18:22). When Zacchaeus was saved, he gave half his goods to the poor (Luke 19:8). Barnabas sold a field and put the money at the feet of the apostles (Acts 4:37). The poor widow put two pennies in the offering box and was commended by Jesus (Luke 21:1–3). C. S. Lewis recommended that we give until it hurts, that we give until we feel the pinch in our lifestyle and our choices. Our generosity ought to be a glorious and costly thing. Nevertheless, for each of us, the amount may vary, but the commitment to use our resources to meet the needs of others is the same.

Giving More Than Money

Doing good and being rich in good works and being generous and ready to share aren't just about money. Too often we limit generosity to writing checks. But wealth is more than money. We ought to be generous with our time and our efforts and our talents and our skills. Even if your bank account is empty, God has still enriched you in all kinds of ways so that you can be generous in all kinds of ways so that thanksgiving would be offered to God for all kinds of reasons. So be creative in how you think about what God has given you and how your life can be poured out for the sake of others.

Let me try to get very concrete here by focusing on your family. Throughout this book, I've been arguing that God reveals himself in everything, that everything is an invitation to know God. Every good and perfect gift comes down from the Father of lights, and every good and perfect gift is meant to lead us back to the Father of lights. The beams come down for our enjoyment, and our enjoyment is meant to lead us back to God. This means that your family—your spouse, your kids, your parents, and your siblings—are gifts that are meant to lead you to God. And as we saw in chapter 3, it also means that you are meant to be a gift from God to them. You are a made thing designed to make invisible attributes visible.

So try this: do you remember the baptism of Jesus in Matthew 3? Jesus comes out of the water, the Spirit descends like a dove, and the Father says, "This is my beloved Son, with whom I am well pleased" (3:17). In this moment we catch a glimpse of the infinite and eternal life of the triune God. Fatherly delight, fatherly joy, fatherly pleasure. And because of the gospel, because we are united to Christ by faith, this joy includes us. God embraces us and delights in us in the same way that he does Jesus, because we have trusted in Jesus. Now, my question is: Will my sons have categories for the glory of that gospel reality? Will there be personal, relational, and spiritual weight to that gospel truth? When they grow up and come to understand Matthew 3 and the Father's delight in his Son, I want them to say, "I get it. I've seen my dad look at me that way. I have categories for fatherly pleasure that echo this gospel of grace. My dad was present for me. My dad spoke words of life and joy and love over me. He gave visible and tangible expressions of his pleasure. He called me his own. I have lived my life beneath the smile of a happy father, and if that fatherly joy is a faint echo of this eternal fatherly joy, then sign me up." I want my wife to read Isaiah 62:5—"As the bridegroom rejoices over the bride, so shall your God rejoice over you"—and say, "My husband still looks at me that way." I want to give my family the gift of a true and glorious picture of what God is like. I want them to experience my joy in God as I delight in them. I want to be the smile of God to my children. I want to be the smile of God to my wife.

I can't tell you how many times I've been driving home from work in a fog of exhaustion, and what keeps me from coming in the house and burdening my family with my frustrated, spent, and heavy presence is the knowledge that as I walk in the door, I will either tell the truth about fatherly delight and husbandly joy, or I will lie. I find that grace floods me in that moment, and I dance up the sidewalk and throw my sons in the air with a tickle fight and ask my wife how I can relieve her of burden. In other words, I enter my house eager to do good, to be rich in good works, to be generous and ready to share my time, my presence, and my affection.

Gladly Spend and Be Spent

Let me close this chapter by showing how these two dimensions—the enjoyment of God's provision and generosity with God's provision—can come together. In 2 Corinthians Paul expresses his plans to visit the Corinthians for the third time:

> Here for the third time I am ready to come to you. And I will not be a burden, for I seek not what is yours but you. For children are not obligated to save up for their parents, but parents for their children. I will most gladly spend and be spent for your souls. (12:14–15)

Do you see both elements? Spend and be spent—that's generosity. Sacrifice, self-denial, pouring ourselves out as we seek to do good and be open-handed with our families and our friends and our neighbors. That's Paul's vision of parenting and Paul's vision of ministry. But notice how he's spending himself. All of his sacrifices are done "most gladly" because he's also receiving the Corinthians as a gift. He doesn't want their stuff; he wants *them*. Paul is receiving them as a gift from God, richly provided to him for his enjoyment. And in receiving them in that way, he is also giving them a gift, the gift of apostolic and fatherly gladness, which is an echo of God's delight offered to us in the gospel.

And when you do this, when you set your hope on God, and you enjoy what he richly provides, and you share what he richly provides, you are storing up treasure for yourself. You save up and you gladly spend it. You store it up and you pour it out. This is the true life; this is the true foundation for the future, the true foundation of everlasting joy.

6

When the Things of
Earth Are Lost

Self-denial is the voluntary giving up of good things for the sake of better things. Generosity is the voluntary giving of good things to others in the cause of love. They are the voluntary ways that we test our enjoyment of the things of earth. It's the voluntary way we show that Jesus is better. But what about the involuntary loss of good gifts? What about when good and precious gifts that expand our capacities to know and enjoy God are ripped from our hearts? What does an integrated approach to the enjoyment of God and his gifts say when the gift is being torn from our hands? That's what this chapter is about—suffering, pain, death.

None of us want to talk about suffering. But we *need* to talk about suffering. I have no doubt that some readers of this book are practically suffocating in the midst of grief and loss. For some of you, the darkness is so thick that the very notion of enjoying God and his gifts is almost inconceivable.

I remember a brief conversation I had with John Piper when I was writing *The Things of Earth*.[7] I was explaining to him the concept of integrated joy—let joy in the gifts soar because it carries joy in God with it. And he nodded and then said, "Until you die. Until you lose them." It was a very Piper thing to say. It was also a very biblical thing to say. If our theology of the things of earth is silent when the baby dies or the persecution comes or the cancer returns, we don't have the right theology. So we have to face the inevitability of losing the good things that are designed to enlarge our minds and hearts to know God. What do we do when precious things of earth are ripped from our hands and torn from our hearts?

Anchoring Our Reflections

In order to focus this chapter, I want to anchor my reflections to a particular section of Scripture. I've chosen 2 Corinthians 1:3–11 because it speaks to the reality of suffering with such clarity and relevance. Before continuing, I want to invite you to read the passage carefully:

> Blessed be the God and Father of our Lord Jesus Christ, the Father of mercies and God of all comfort, who comforts us in all our affliction, so that we may be able to comfort those who are in any affliction, with the comfort with which we ourselves are comforted by God. For as we share abundantly in Christ's sufferings, so through Christ we share abundantly in comfort too. If we are afflicted, it is for your comfort and salvation; and if we are comforted, it is for your comfort, which you experience when you patiently endure the same sufferings that we suffer. Our hope for you is unshaken, for we know that as you share in our sufferings, you will also share in our comfort. For we do

not want you to be unaware, brothers, of the affliction we experienced in Asia. For we were so utterly burdened beyond our strength that we despaired of life itself. Indeed, we felt that we had received the sentence of death. But that was to make us rely not on ourselves but on God who raises the dead. He delivered us from such a deadly peril, and he will deliver us. On him we have set our hope that he will deliver us again. You also must help us by prayer, so that many will give thanks on our behalf for the blessing granted us through the prayers of many. (2 Cor. 1:3–11)

With that passage in mind, let's start by distinguishing different *kinds* of suffering. We might distinguish natural suffering (such as sickness and disease) and moral suffering (such as persecution and malice). We could distinguish suffering based on intensity—inconveniences (such as when your favorite restaurant changes its menu and drops your favorite item) versus calamities (such as the death of a loved one). For the purposes of this chapter, I'm going to focus mainly on natural suffering (not persecution) and on calamities (not inconveniences). But within the category of natural calamities, there is another distinction I want to make. It's the difference between losing something that we already had and desiring something that we've not received. This is the suffering of *loss* and the suffering of *longing*. Both are painful. Both can break your heart. But there are differences worth noting.

In the suffering of loss, we know the sweetness of what we no longer possess. When Dad dies, when the child dies, when sickness or injury robs us of health, we hurt because we know what we're missing. Our past haunts our present. We look back and say, "Why? God, why did you take him? Why did this happen to me?"

89

In the suffering of longing, we hurt because we want something that God is withholding. It's not that he's taking; it's that he's not giving. When we're longing for a husband or a wife, when we're aching for a baby, our future haunts our present. We look around and say, "Why not? God, why not me?"

Now, I bring up these distinctions in kinds of suffering for a reason. They matter. The particulars matter. In 2 Corinthians 1 Paul says that he doesn't want them to be unaware of the affliction in Asia—the unbearable burden, the despair, the feeling that they had been sentenced to die. The Asian affliction was different from the Syrian affliction or the Thessalonian affliction. There are differences between loss and longing, and between losing a parent and losing a child, between wanting a spouse and wanting a baby. The particulars do matter.

But the main reason I bring up the distinctions is the danger of the distinctions. It is far too easy for us to compare suffering, to try and gauge who has suffered more or whose pain lingers longest. It's easy to look at the affliction in Asia and say that it's worse than the affliction in Corinth. It's easy for the unmarried to look at the pains of marriage and say, "At least you have a spouse." It's easy for someone who has lost a child to look at the loss of a sibling or parent and say, "It's not the same." And that's true. It's not the same. The particulars matter. But that truth can actually hide one of the central things that the Bible wants us to see about suffering. Listen again to Paul's words in 2 Corinthians:

> Blessed be the God and Father of our Lord Jesus Christ, the Father of mercies and God of all comfort, who comforts us in all our affliction, so that we may be able to comfort those who are in any affliction, with the comfort with which we ourselves are comforted by God. (1:3–4)

God comforts us in *our* affliction, so that we may be able to comfort those in *any* affliction. There are different afflictions, and those differences matter. But we cannot let the differences in affliction overshadow the fundamental commonality in all afflictions. What is that commonality? It's that the only comfort in any and all affliction comes from the one God, the Father of mercies and God of all comfort. *All* comfort. Whether you've lost someone or you're longing for someone. Whether you're assaulted by sickness or assaulted by evil men. Whether your suffering is comparatively great or comparatively small. Our only hope in affliction comes from the only God who gives all comfort.

Effects of Suffering

Let's look now at effects of suffering. I have three effects in mind. The first is *guilt*. That may sound odd to some, but for Christians who believe that the steadfast love of the Lord is better than life and who confess that all things are loss compared to knowing Jesus, guilt in the midst of suffering is real. When the calamity occurs, when the pain and loss run deep, when the sorrow doesn't go away, there can be, in the back of the mind, a low-grade guilt. "If I really trusted God, if I really loved him above all else, I wouldn't hurt this way. It wouldn't cut me this deep." And the effect of that guilt is to push us away from the God of all comfort. We can't deny our sorrow, and since we feel that our sorrow shows how little we love God, we run from God. We isolate ourselves from him.

And not only from him. The second effect is *isolation*. There arises between the sufferer and the world an invisible blanket. The comparison that I mentioned earlier can feed this. "They don't understand. They've not suffered as I have." People and relationships are hard when we're hurting. They don't know what to say. We don't know what to say. Everyone feels embarrassed and awkward. We can't speak of it. We can't not speak of it. Best to just go our separate ways.

The final effect I have in mind is *anger and frustration*. Anger at God. Frustration at the world. Why did he do this? Why didn't he stop this? And this anger at God can increase both the guilt and the isolation. We find that our anger at God bubbles out in strange ways. We're angry at him for letting this happen to us, but we can't do anything to get back at him directly. So we end up taking it out on other people. We lash out at others and this further isolates us from the very people who might be able to offer comfort.

This anger and frustration is compounded when the God of all comfort seems absent in our pain. Like Paul, we feel the despair and hopelessness of being abandoned by God. C. S. Lewis captures this well in writing about the death of his wife:

> Meanwhile, where is God? This is one of the most disquieting symptoms. When you are happy, so happy that you have no sense of needing Him, so happy that you are tempted to feel His claims upon you as an interruption, if you remember yourself and turn to Him with gratitude and praise, you will be—or so it feels—welcomed with open arms. But go to Him when your need is desperate, when all other help is vain, and what do you find? A door slammed in your face, and a sound of bolting and double bolting on the inside. After that, silence. You may as well turn away. The longer you wait, the more emphatic the silence will become. There are no lights in the windows. It might be an empty house. Was it ever inhabited? It seemed so once. And that seeming was as strong as this. What can this mean? Why is He so present

a commander in our time of prosperity and so very absent a help in time of trouble?[8]

Lewis goes on to say that the real danger for many of us at this point is not that we would cease to believe in God. Rather, it's that we come to believe such dreadful things about him. "This is what God is *really* like. He wounds us and then won't heal. He wrecks us and then turns his back. This affliction might be bearable if I knew he was near, but I don't feel his nearness." And this distrust is worse than unbelief. We believe in God, but he has become a horror to us. We look back on his graciousness as preparation for his next torture (and we imagine that keeping our distance from him will somehow be a protection). Paul says, "He delivered us in the past; he will deliver us again." We say, "He has afflicted us in the past, and he will afflict us again." In fact, these horrible thoughts are often a way for us to get back at God in the only way we can. We cannot actually injure him, so we call him a cosmic sadist and believe lies about him—that he is cruel and uncaring and harsh. And between the guilt ("Does my pain show that I have loved the gift too much?") and the isolation ("No one understands") and the anger ("God is cruel and uncaring"), we spiral into deeper despair and bitterness and grief. This is the reality of suffering that we all must face.

Purposes in Suffering

Before I give some practical responses to these effects of suffering, it will be good to see the purposes of suffering in light of what we've seen in this book about enjoying the things of earth. First, suffering, whether of loss or of longing, is the ultimate comparative test for our joy in God and his gifts. It forces us to put our money where our mouth is. We sing, "Hallelujah, all I have is Christ!" And then God asks if we mean it. Is he enough? If you lose everything, and all you have is Jesus, is he enough?

We see this again and again in the Bible. Friends abandon us in our time of need. Will we be undone? Or will we be like Paul?

> At my first defense no one came to stand by me, but all deserted me. May it not be charged against them! But the Lord stood by me and strengthened me, so that through me the message might be fully proclaimed and all the Gentiles might hear it. So I was rescued from the lion's mouth. The Lord will rescue me from every evil deed and bring me safely into his heavenly kingdom. To him be the glory forever and ever. Amen. (2 Tim. 4:16–18)

If our parents reject us and forsake us, can we say with the psalmist, "My father and my mother have forsaken me, but the LORD will take me in" (Ps. 27:10)?

When the storm comes and blows the house down with our children inside it, will we curse God or say with Job, "The LORD gave, and the LORD has taken away; blessed be the name of the LORD" (Job 1:21)? Or when all sources of earthly joy and prosperity fail, can we say what Habakkuk says?

> Though the fig tree should not blossom,
>   nor fruit be on the vines,
> the produce of the olive fail
>   and the fields yield no food,
> the flock be cut off from the fold
>   and there be no herd in the stalls,
> yet I will rejoice in the LORD;
>   I will take joy in the God of my salvation.
>   (Hab. 3:17–18)

Here's a good exercise for all of us. Take Habakkuk 3 and personalize it. What things of earth are sources of deep joy and stability and prosperity in your life? Put them in place of fig trees and flocks, and try praying this to the Lord.

So suffering tests whether God is supreme in our hearts and minds. It's the comparative approach in action. But what about integrated joy? What about enjoying God in everything and everything in God? Does it go when the gift goes? Is suffering only about the comparative approach? I don't think so. Integrated joy continues even in the absence of the gift. To see how, you have to remember that the heart of enjoying everything in God is soul expansion. The things of earth enlarge our minds and hearts so that we can know God more. And this soul expansion happens when the gift is present, and it can happen when the gift is absent.

A number of years ago some of our closest friends lost their son. He was born with a terminal birth defect and died at six months old. I remember trying to be with them in their suffering. And I remember thinking, "If I were in their shoes, I might have a hitch in my grief because of my belief in the sovereignty of God. If God is taking the baby, then am I fighting him because I want to keep the baby here as long as possible? Am I loving this baby too much?" I didn't know whether they were feeling that, but I wrote them a short note and said, "I know you guys love Jesus above everything. And so I just wanted to say, you can't love your son too much. It is impossible for you to feel too deeply for him, for you to want to hold him too much, for you to long and ache for him with too much intensity."

Now how could I say that? Was I saying that idolatry was impossible for the grieving? Not at all. But idolatry isn't loving something too much. It's loving something *in place of God*. You only love wrongly when you separate the gift from the giver and love the gift instead of God. But if you receive the gift, if you receive your son as a gift from God, then you cannot love him too much or prize him too highly. Love for your son (and grief over the impending loss) is what love for God looks like when the Lord gives the son and then the Lord takes away.

Responses to Suffering

The paradigm set forth in this book is designed to help us respond rightly when affliction comes. Because it will come. And when it does, there are three things we must do. First, we must press into the pain. We must not stand aloof and detached. We're not Stoics. We don't believe the lie that says, "If you truly loved God, you wouldn't be weeping and wailing like this." Instead we grieve the way that people in the Bible grieved. Job trusted in the goodness of God, and that didn't keep him from feeling the loss of his children. He tore his robe. He shaved his head. He fell on the ground, and he sat there for seven days. He grieved and wept and worshiped through tears.

Or just read the Psalms. Listen to David and Asaph wrestle with God in their grief. "How long, O LORD? Will you forget me forever?" (Ps. 13:1). "Why do you hide yourself in times of trouble?" (Ps. 10:1). They cry out for justice. They claim his promises. They hold nothing back. They pour out their souls to God.

And then, of course, there's Jesus. Man of sorrows and acquainted with grief. Weeping over Jerusalem. Deeply moved in his spirit by the grief of Mary and Martha. Shedding troubled tears at the tomb of Lazarus, minutes before he would raise him from the dead.

Now, why can they do this? Why can they (and we) press into the pain? In 2013 my dad passed away after a seven-year battle with dementia and Parkinson's. At some point during those years, I came across a quotation that has hung with me ever since. "It hurts just as much as it's worth." It hurts just as much as *he's* worth. It hurts just as much as *she's* worth. Sorrow is what love looks like when love's object is taken. The depth of the pain shows the value of what was lost. And the whole point of this book has been that the things of earth are unfathomably valuable because they are designed to bring us to God. And they can bring us to him, even when they are being taken by him.

This was my word to my friend when he was watching his son die:

> I just want to encourage you to plunge headlong into the gift. Savor every moment with your son. Touch him, hold him, caress him, let the love that you feel for him surge through you. Let it provoke you to tears and sadness and that gut-wrenching feeling that you would do absolutely *anything* to make your son whole. Let your love for your little boy take you beyond the pain and sorrow to the indestructible joy of the God who gives good gifts *and is not threatened by them.*
>
> It's as if God is saying to you, "You don't know how intense my love is for you, how deep my affections are for you. So I'm going to show you. I'm going to stretch your heart to the breaking point. It will feel like you are dying. But if you go with me, into the love, into the pain, into the sorrow and longing and desire, then when all is said and done, you will know that as a father has compassion on his children, so does the Lord have compassion on you."

Second, we must press into people. We must not isolate ourselves. It may hurt more. They may not know what to say. It may be embarrassing. In addition to the loss, we may have to endure the additional pain of being pitied. No one likes to be pitied.

In 2 Corinthians the central link between the God of all comfort and the afflicted person is others who have suffered and been comforted. We are one of the key ways that God brings comfort. It's our prayers that bring help. It's our presence and words that bring comfort. But bringing comfort to others requires that we have received comfort ourselves and have the wisdom to know how to channel that comfort in ways that will actually help.

We need wisdom about when to speak and when to be silent, when to sit and grieve and when to offer counsel. We need wisdom to know *who* should speak and what words are appropriate and when those words are appropriate. And we need grace and patience from those who are afflicted when we fail. Who is sufficient for these things? But the fact that it is hard doesn't mean that we can avoid it. We're the link between the comfort of Christ and the affliction of people. If we're to do 2 Corinthians 1 well, we must be connected *both* to the one who is afflicted and to the God of all comfort.

Finally, we must press into the Lord. In your sorrow, do not sin. Weep, wail, grieve, lament. Rage against this broken and cursed world and the evil powers that steal and kill and destroy. But never curse God. Don't run from him. He is the only source of comfort. He is the God of all comfort. Press on to know him. Press hard into him. As surely as the coming of the dawn, he will respond.

For me, songs and poetry can often communicate better than a sermon or a chapter. One of my favorites is an old hymn entitled "Come, Ye Disconsolate." Here are the lyrics:

Come, ye disconsolate, where'er ye languish;
come to the mercy seat, fervently kneel.

Here bring your wounded hearts, here tell your anguish;
earth has no sorrows that heaven cannot heal.

Joy of the desolate, light of the straying,
hope of the penitent, fadeless and pure!
Here speaks the Comforter, in mercy saying,
"Earth has no sorrows that heaven cannot cure."

Here see the bread of life; see waters flowing
forth from the throne of God, pure from above.
Come to the feast prepared; come, ever knowing
earth has no sorrows but heaven can remove.[9]

I love that hymn because of the last line of each verse. God never takes without giving back. He brings us face-to-face with death so that we will rely not on ourselves but on the God who raises the dead. The sufferings of this present time are not worth comparing to the glory to be revealed. These light and momentary afflictions are working for us an eternal weight of glory that far outweighs them all. Nothing good will ever finally be lost. Earth has no sorrows that heaven cannot heal.

7

Treasure in the Field

In this final chapter, I want to get personal. I want to try to draw the various threads of this book together in a personal case study drawn from my own life. I've chosen baseball because, for me, baseball is a thick joy, a complex joy with many layers. As we've seen, some joys are simple and direct. You eat honey, and you go straight to God. Honey is good. God is good. Simple. But other joys are complex and interwoven and take us deeper into the world and into our experiences and our past before they take us godward. So I'm not necessarily aiming to win you to my delight in baseball (though if that happens, I won't complain). Instead, I want to use my particular joy in baseball to illustrate the truths in this book.

Enjoying the Perfect Game

As I said, baseball is a thick joy for me. First, there is the physical aspect. Running, throwing, hitting, catching, coaching—all of these require physical effort and skill, which engage us as embodied beings. And physical training is of some value.

Second, there's the recreational aspect. Baseball, like many sports, provides a respite from the cares and burdens of life. I breathe easier on the baseball diamond. Third, there's a philosophical aspect. As David Bentley Hart argues in a wonderful essay, baseball is "a perfect game."[10] In fact, Hart says that baseball may be America's greatest contribution to the history of civilization. An audacious claim like that requires some explanation.

Hart begins by noting that baseball is distinct from most other sports, which are basically about moving a ball from one end of the court or field or pitch to the other in order to score more goals or points than the other team before time runs out. Football, basketball, soccer, hockey, lacrosse—all are variations of this basic game, with the differences lying in the size or shape of the ball and the part of the body (or equipment) that is used to move it. Baseball is different. There's no clock, only twenty-seven outs, which means, as Yogi Berra famously said, "It ain't over till it's over." As long as there is one out, one strike left, anything can happen.

Moreover, Hart notes the exact fittingness of the dimensions: 90 feet between the bases, and 60 feet and 6 inches from the rubber to the plate. Everything so exquisitely timed that a ball fielded cleanly in the infield is almost always an out, but a slight bobble is almost always a hit.

It's a team sport with a decidedly individualistic bent, as pitcher and batter stare each other down with little to no help from anyone else. There are the tactics and strategies that change from inning to inning and pitch to pitch. Baseball taps into the movement of the seasons—from the promising brightness of spring training to the dog days of summer to the intensity of autumn, as well as the knowledge that all good things come to an end (at least, until pitchers and catchers report).

As Hart also notes, baseball is a child's game that recalls for us the innocence of Eden, with the ballpark standing as a carefully cultivated garden that enchants the young and makes old hearts new again. And, Hart adds, baseball also recalls the intrusion of evil into paradise, whenever the Yankees come to town. And, if I could add a biblical reflection of my own, the three bases and home plate have always reminded me of the Levitical cities of refuge, where the manslayer is safe from the avenger of blood who seeks to dispatch him to Sheol (or to the dugout). These be deep matters, and the philosophically inclined among us have much to ponder in America's pastime.

Fourth, there's a social dimension to the enjoyment—the teamwork, the shared training that builds brotherhood and camaraderie. Relational and vocational pleasures come together as nine players work together to prepare for the season, or start a two-out rally, or end a two-out rally, or relay a throw to the plate.

Fifth, for me, there's a multifaceted familial dimension. My grandfather played and managed in the majors. My dad worked in the front office for minor league teams. My father-in-law has been a baseball fan since he was a boy growing up in New York, and he not only carried that passion into adulthood but faithfully imparted it to his children (and now his grandchildren). There's the bonding with my boys as I practice and play with them in the front yard. And there's a nostalgic dimension for me now, as I coach my boys and remember my childhood when my dad taught me to throw and hit and I played in the front yard with my brothers.

Finally, there's a bittersweet dimension, because in 2013, we buried my dad after a seven-year battle with dementia, and I miss him most on the baseball diamond. I wish he could see my boys play. In short, for me, baseball is a thickly woven thing of earth.

How Natural Joys Become Joys in God

Now, joy in baseball is a natural joy. There is nothing inherently spiritual about it. Millions of players and fans enjoy the game with no supernatural or spiritual dimension at all. But this is a book about enjoying God in everything and everything in God. So how does my natural joy in baseball become a supernatural joy in God? That's the question Christian Hedonists ask. There are hundreds of answers to it. I'll give four.

1. BASEBALL TRAINS FUTURE MEN.

Joy in playing and coaching baseball becomes joy in God when I recognize that physical training has some value, including value as a picture of training in godliness (1 Tim. 4:8). A significant part of that value is in raising boys to become men. Baseball, like many sports, creates the opportunity for channeling masculinity in fruitful directions. Baseball awakens ambition, competition, the drive for excellence, intense emotions in victory and defeat. These are all good, but dangerous. Coaching my sons in baseball is an opportunity to train them to master these emotions and to cultivate humility, patience, diligence, perseverance, and joy in all circumstances. Such habits of natural virtue and self-mastery are a crucial part of growth in maturity and have real and lasting value in cultivating spiritual virtue and godliness.

2. BASEBALL ALLOWS ME TO EXPRESS
GOD'S HEART TO MY SONS.

Joy in baseball becomes joy in God when I share joy with my sons and therefore love them by showing them what God is like. We know the distinct delight of introducing another person to one of our favorite pleasures. The pleasure of sharing is distinct in kind from the pleasure of the object or activity. It's one thing to enjoy reading a book I love; it's another flavor of joy to give that book to my son whom I expect will also love it, and then find that he does. The anticipation of sharing that story with him, of seeing him light up at the same parts, of entering into the joy for the first time, is its own reward. This is often what parents are—the bringers and introducers of joys.

God is like that. He loves to be the bringer of joys. One reason he made the universe is so that there could be some third thing that he could bring to us, eyes aflame with knowing expectation, and say, "Here you go. Try it."

We catch a glimpse of this in the creation of Eve—Adam's solitude, God's recognition that it's not good, the failed attempt at finding a helper among the beasts, and then the deep sleep, the awakening, the triumphant "At last!" I can't help but picture God with a knowing grin as he builds the woman from Adam's rib. He pictures the scene when Adam awakes; he anticipates Adam's euphoria in the same way that parents anticipate their children's joy on Christmas Eve as they place the presents around the tree.

I know it's an analogy; God is, after all, simple and timeless, without shadow of turning (or anticipation). Whatever likeness there is between my experience as the bringer of joy to my sons and God's experience of bringing joy to us, there is also a great unlikeness, because God is not in time, God is not complex,

God does not anticipate, God does not change. But despite that unlikeness, I believe that the likeness is real. My joy in sharing baseball with my boys is something like God's joy in sharing everything with me (including baseball).

3. BASEBALL HELPS ME TOWARD HOLINESS.

Joy in baseball becomes joy in God when it helps me to kill sin and pursue holiness. When I'm on the field, I find that my burdens lift. There's a much-needed respite from the pressures of life and ministry, an echo of Eden, which I deliberately wield in the fight of faith. When I'm shaping my boys into men and sharing joy with them and showing them what God is like, I'm doing what I was made for. So, in coaching, I feel God's pleasure. And in feeling God's pleasure, I put my sin to death. I'm a better husband, a better father, a better pastor. When I wield baseball in the fight for holiness, joy in baseball becomes joy in God.

4. BASEBALL POINTS ME TO THE WORLD TO COME.

The bittersweetness of my dad's absence brings a note of earthly sorrow and heavenly hope into the present joy. In other words, my sorrow on the field points me forward to the day when sorrows and sighings flee away. My sadness because of my dad's absence on that baseball field is a reminder of the coming day when, as Tolkien said, everything sad comes untrue.

I sometimes imagine heaven as a Little League baseball game, with my boys playing, me coaching, and my dad watching. It's a joy I'll never have on earth. I don't know that I'll have it in heaven. I have no idea how the distinct joy of playing catch with a seven-year-old while being watched by a seventy-year-old could be there. How old will we be in heaven?

A mother knows that the pleasure of holding her newborn is one of the highest joys of her life. But how can there be newborns in heaven? And isn't my heavenly baseball game just like a barren woman who pictures herself in heaven rocking a newborn to sleep? What is the point of imagining such impossibilities?

But in my case, the heavenly ball game is not what I really want. The ball game is a placeholder for something. It's a way of reaffirming my belief in Revelation 21:4—"He will wipe away every tear from [my] eyes." It's my way of believing the promises of God.

But, you might say, God didn't promise me the baseball game with my sons and my dad. That's true. But he did promise, "No good thing does he withhold from those who walk uprightly" (Ps. 84:11). "He who did not spare his own Son but gave him up for us all, how will he not also with him graciously give us all things?" (Rom. 8:32).

All things, including the baseball game and the barren woman's child. Heaven will have either my ball game or something better. Heaven will see the barren woman with either a baby or something better. But since I have no clear picture of what the "something better" might be, I project my greatest desires (which are often the converse of my greatest earthly sorrows), and then say, "Even better than that."

Make Imagination Serve Your Joy

So, you see, the exercise is not in vain. The fact that the mind of man has not conceived what God has prepared for those who love him doesn't mean that we shouldn't exercise our mental muscles, just as the fact that the love of Christ surpasses knowledge doesn't mean that we should cease trying to know it. Pushing the limits of our conceptions (provided we remember that they are only our conceptions) doesn't threaten the joys of heaven. No one will be disappointed, least of all me. We work out our imaginations here so that we can, metaphorically speaking, give God's omnipotent goodness a workout there.

So joys in the things of earth become joys in God when they are:

1. received and recognized as pictures of spiritual reality and on-ramps to spiritual virtue;
2. shared with others as a way of loving them;
3. wielded as a weapon in the fight of faith; and
4. enjoyed (or grieved) as a way of anticipating the joys of the new heaven and the new earth.

And that's just a sample. There are countless variations and combinations of earthly joys, custom-made for each one of us, all designed as invitations from God to know and delight in him. Each joy individually, and all earthly joys together, are calling us to go further up and higher in to the life of the God of all pleasure.

When enjoyed rightly, they transform the idolatry and ingratitude of Romans 1 into the thanksgiving and adoration of the renewed heart. Every good and perfect gift comes down from the Father, and every good and perfect gift is designed to lead us back to the Father of lights, in whose presence is fullness of joy and at whose right hand are pleasures forevermore.

Epilogue

As we come to the end of this book, I'm mindful of its shortcomings. So many subjects left untreated. So many questions left unanswered. If you'd like to explore this topic further, you might want to read the larger book I mentioned earlier, *The Things of Earth: Treasuring God by Enjoying His Gifts*, which goes into much greater detail. It's about three times the size of this book and lays a deeper theological foundation, explores more biblical passages, answers a wider variety of questions, and offers more practical guidance and advice for living out this vision of the Christian life.[11]

For now, I simply want to close with a basic summary of this book and one simple piece of advice. The living God made the world so that we could know him. He reveals himself to us in creation and in Scripture, in his world and in his word. Everything in creation declares his glory. Made things make his invisible attributes visible. All of God's gifts are invitations—they display who he is and invite us to know him and delight in him. They are the beams; he is the sun. They are the streams; he is the fountain. So our calling is simple: to enjoy God in everything and everything in God, knowing that he is greater and more satisfying than any and all of his gifts. Jesus is better. At a practical level, this means that we anchor ourselves in his word and orient ourselves in worship and then carry the divine presence with us into our daily lives. As made things that make things, we too ought to display the glory of God and invite people to know him and enjoy him. We do this by gratefully receiving all that he richly provides and by joyfully sacrificing and sharing all that we have received. Even as we receive the gifts, we deny ourselves daily and gladly spend our wealth and our time and ourselves in loving others so that they too can be supremely happy in God.

That's the summary. Now here's the advice. Begin where you are. Whatever earthly things are present to you now, start with them. Whether it's warm sunshine or a cool spring rain. Whether it's eating enchiladas or sipping lemonade. Whether it's planning a project for work or having a conversation with your spouse. Whether it's working in the yard or wrestling with your kids. Whatever good and perfect gifts are coming down to you now from the Father of lights, begin with them. Receive them with gratitude. Savor them with gladness. Study them with delight. Share them with others. And refuse to stop with the gifts. Follow them back to the giver. See them as declarations of his glory. Know them as images of divine things. And then turn your eyes upon Jesus. Look full in his wonderful face. And the things of earth will grow strangely *bright*, in the light of his glory and grace.

Appendix

Since writing *The Things of Earth*, the most common criticism I've received is that for all of my detailed descriptions and lavish praise of my wife's pumpkin crunch cake, I failed to include the recipe in the book. Understandably, some have regarded this as a serious defect in my writing. Happily, this book affords me the opportunity to rectify that mistake. So without further ado, here is the recipe for my wife's world-famous pumpkin crunch cake.

Pumpkin Crunch Cake

Ingredients

1 can (15 oz.) pumpkin
1 can (12 fl. oz.) evaporated milk
1-1/2 cups granulated sugar
2 tsp. pumpkin pie spice
1 tsp. salt
4 eggs
1/2 box yellow cake mix
1 cup chopped pecans
1 cup unsalted butter

Directions

Preheat oven to 350 degrees. Beat together first six ingredients until well mixed and pour into 9 x 13–inch greased pan. Sprinkle 1/2 box of yellow cake mix over pumpkin mixture. Then sprinkle chopped pecans over cake mix. Thinly slice butter over pecans (use entire cup, or more, if needed to completely cover the cake). Bake for 50–55 minutes. Enjoy with vanilla ice cream or whipped cream!

Notes

1. C. S. Lewis, *Letters to Malcolm: Chiefly on Prayer* (San Diego: Harcourt, Brace, 1992), 75.
2. Jonathan Edwards, *Typological Writings*, vol. 11, *The Works of Jonathan Edwards*, ed. Wallace E. Anderson, Mason I. Lowance, and David H. Watters (New Haven, CT: Yale University Press, 1993), 152.
3. Joe Rigney, "Christian Hedonism and the Things of Earth," Bethlehem College & Seminary website, February 4, 2019, https://bcsmn.edu /archive-video/christian-hedonism-and-the-things-of-earth/.
4. David Mathis, *Habits of Grace: Enjoying Jesus through the Spiritual Disciplines* (Wheaton, IL: Crossway, 2016).
5. C. S. Lewis, *Perelandra* (New York: HarperOne, 2012), 43–44.
6. C. S. Lewis, *Out of the Silent Planet* (New York: HarperOne, 2012), 74.
7. Joe Rigney, *The Things of Earth: Treasuring God by Enjoying His Gifts* (Wheaton, IL: Crossway, 2015).
8. C. S. Lewis, *A Grief Observed* (New York: HarperOne, 1996), 4.
9. "Come Ye Disconsolate, Where'er Ye Languish," Thomas Moore (1816), rev. Thomas Hastings (1832).
10. David Bentley Hart, "A Perfect Game: The Metaphysical Meaning of Baseball," *First Things* (August 2010): https://www.firstthings.com /article/2010/08/a-perfect-game.
11. Rigney, *The Things of Earth*.

General Index

115

Scripture Index

Scripture Index

How do we develop a love for the things of earth and a deep love for God?

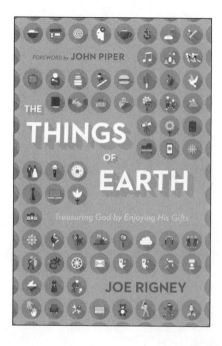

Helping us avoid our tendency to forget the Giver on the one hand and neglect his gifts on the other, *The Things of Earth* reminds us that God's blessings should drive us to worship and that a passion for God's glory can be as wide as the world itself.

"Reading this will be a sweet moment of profound liberation for many. With wisdom and verve, Rigney shows how we can worship our creator through the enjoyment of his creation."

MICHAEL REEVES, President and Professor of Theology, Union School of Theology, Oxford, United Kingdom

For more information, visit **crossway.org**.

"Many of us are illiterate when it comes to reading anything other than a book. Joe follows Scripture's example by teaching us how to read the world, the creation, and the gifts of God under the authority of the word of God. This is an important book, and I hope you'll read it."

Abigail Dodds, author, *(A)Typical Woman: Free, Whole, and Called in Christ*

"God's passion for his glory and our ache to be truly happy are not at odds but rather one life-changing pursuit. And so too with God himself and the world he made—not at odds but rather God means for us to enjoy him in everything, and everything in him. It sounds so simple, but in our finitude and fallenness, we are so prone to get tripped up over this. For years, Joe Rigney has handled this dilemma as well as anyone I'm aware of, and now he does it with even more focus and accessibility. I've eagerly awaited this short book with its life-changing vision, and I could hardly be more excited that it's finally here."

David Mathis, Executive Editor, desiringGod.org; Pastor, Cities Church, St. Paul, Minnesota; author, *Habits of Grace: Enjoying Jesus through the Spiritual Disciplines*

"Since Constantine entered Rome in October of AD 312 and ended Christian persecution, the faithful have struggled with their embrace of God and their love for the world. Instead of gladiator games, it's UFC. Instead of pagan celebrations, it's Netflix binging and secularized holidays. How can Christians in the twenty-first century enjoy the world without sacrificing their primary obligation to love the Lord? Joe Rigney provides remarkably timely advice on enjoying God's creation while still putting God above his creation."

Erick-Woods Erickson, Editor, *The Resurgent*